SELECTED POEMS
OF
THOMAS HARDY

SELECTED POEMS
OF
THOMAS HARDY

Edited
with an Introduction by
G. M. YOUNG

MACMILLAN AND CO., LIMITED
ST. MARTIN'S STREET, LONDON
1953

—

First Edition 1940
First printed in The Golden Treasury Series 1950
Reprinted 1953

MACMILLAN AND COMPANY LIMITED
London Bombay Calcutta Madras Melbourne

THE MACMILLAN COMPANY OF CANADA LIMITED
Toronto

ST MARTIN'S PRESS INC
New York

PRINTED IN GREAT BRITAIN

CONTENTS

POEMS OF MEMORY AND REFLECTION

INTRODUCTION

I

THE movement of English poetry in the century which followed the appearance of *Lyrical Ballads* may be considered as a succession of three phases, each imparting something of its own character to the next. The poets of the mid-century, Tennyson, Browning and Arnold, were not less affected by the first Romantic group than, in their turn, Rossetti, Swinburne and Morris were affected by their own immediate predecessors. But, as the century approached its end, the springs of poetry began to sink. A frailer and more deliberate art prevailed.

The poetry of the Nineties has a colour and a personality as unmistakable as the sonnet sequences of the last Elizabethan decade. Like them, it was much influenced by foreign examples : it aimed less at originality than accomplishment : and, like them, it could be very tedious. The accomplishment is undeniable. Almost at random — but the quality of this verse is so uniform that it is not easy to go wrong — I take a lyric of John Davidson's :

As I came up from Dymchurch Wall,
  I saw above the Downs' low crest
The crimson brands of sunset fall,
  Flicker and fade from out the west.

Night sank ; like flakes of silver fire
  The stars in one great shower came down ;
Shrill blew the wind ; and shrill the wire
  Rang out from Hythe to Romney town.

> The darkly shining salt sea drops
>> Streamed as the waves clashed on the shore :
> The beach with all its organ stops
>> Pealing again, prolonged the roar.

That is the authentic singing voice of the Nineties. But what is this ? —

> Passing heaths, and the House of Long Sieging,
>> I neared the thin steeple
> That tops the fair fane of Poore's olden
>> Episcopal see ;

> And still sadly onward I followed
>> That Highway the Icen,
> Which trails its pale riband down Wessex
>> By lynchet and lea :

> Along through the Stour-bordered Forum
>> Where Legions had wayfared,
> And where the slow river-face glasses
>> Its green canopy.

This ancient music ? This gnarled and wintry phrasing ?

II

Poetry, let us never forget, is not an affair of the great names only, of the one or two immortal lights. They are only those who have done well what scores of others were doing somehow.

> And one, a foreground black with stones and slags,
>> Beyond, a line of heights, and higher
> All barr'd with long white cloud the scornful crags,
>> And highest, snow and fire.

x

Who, we may ask, but Tennyson could have written so in the Thirties? Well, when the spirit was upon her, Felicia Hemans could:

> And then, a glorious mountain chain uprose,
>   Height above spiry height,
> A soaring solitude of woods and snows,
>   All steeped in golden light.

And is this not Shelley? —

> She kept her own immortal form,
> And I came as the breezes soft and warm
> Of which she breathed. I was a sigh
> Within her heart, alternately
> Coming and going.

No : it is John Banim.

In judging the poets, it is well, therefore, now and then, to take a view of the levels from which they rose, even though the exploration may lead us into those barren places of uninspired cravings and unaccomplished labours which memory rejects and history disdains to record. Never, I suppose, was there such an abundance of versifying as in Victorian England : and when we have turned over a hundred volumes bearing names which prolong a vicarious existence in the handbooks, there remains, untold, forgotten, the vast bulk of occasional verse, fugitive verse : anecdotal, descriptive, reflective, hortatory, hymnodic ; never collected, never reprinted ; magazine poetry, good enough to serve its weekly or monthly turn, and then fade briskly into oblivion : a casual exercise, an agreeable accomplishment, a serious relaxation. Much of Hardy's verse rises no higher.

> The smile on your mouth was the deadest thing
>   Alive enough to have strength to die :
> And a grin of bitterness swept thereby,
>   Like an ominous bird a-wing.
>
> Since then, keen lessons that love deceives,
>   And wrings with wrong, have shaped to me
> Your face, and the God-curst sun, and a tree,
>   And a pond edged with grayish leaves.

So Hardy wrote in 1867. So any young man who had read Browning and Swinburne might have written. It is a copy of verses, nothing more. His work was in the other harmony of prose.

III

Yet to this task, or relaxation, of verse, he brought one gift of rare and curious power. He was steeped in the ancient music of rural England, of song and dance, of psalm and hymn ; of village choir and of harvest-home : and the example of William Barnes was there to show him what could be made of it. The musical inspiration, for example, of the verses quoted above is manifest.

> When sycamore leaves wer a-spreadèn
>   Green-ruddy in hedges,
> Bezide the red doust of the ridges,
>   A-dried at Woak Hill ;

> I packed up my goods, all a-sheenèn
>> Wi' long years o' handlèn,
> On dousty red wheels of a wagon,
>> To ride at Woak Hill.

Barnes, as Hardy said, was a spontaneous singer, but a deliberate artist, " warbling his woodnotes with a watchful eye on the predetermined score," a scholar in many tongues. Hardy's cast of mind was different: his natural powers greater. But without the practice of Barnes before him, it may be doubted whether he would ever have achieved that singular purity of rhythm, that mingling of simplicity and subtlety, which, audible even in his earliest verses, grew with the years, and with increasing mastery of the instrument, into the lyrical triumphs of *The Dynasts*, where every measure, from the most trivial to the most august, is handled with equal aptness and assurance, while again and again the ear can catch, as so often in our native song, echoes of a still older music, borne on the hymns and carols of the Middle Ages, from Provence and far beyond.

We come and learn as time's disordered—deaf sands run,
That Castlereagh's diplomacy has—wiled waxed won.

Companho, non posc mudar qu'eu—nom esfrei
De novellas qu'ai auzidas — e que vei.

In the wild October night-time, when the wind raved round
    the land,
And the Back-sea met the Front-sea, and our doors were
    blocked with sand :

Γλαῦχ', ὅρα, βαθὺς γὰρ ἤδη κύμασιν ταράσσεται
πόντος, ἀμφὶ δ' ἄκρα Γυρέων ὀρθὸν ἵσταται νέφος.

But in the other matter of diction as opposed to music, we may lament that Hardy found no such exemplar. It is doing his fame no service to deny that, of all our writers, he can be, at times, the flattest and the most ungainly. And then, perhaps, we think of Egdon and the Vale of the Great Dairies, and remember, what so many have felt, that craving for Hardy which comes over the exile. The secret, what makes him, some may think, our greatest master in the old pastoral tradition, is the loving precision, the almost professional exactitude with which he specifies those sights — and still more those sounds — of the English landscape, of which we are most conscious when they are not there to be heard or seen. I use the word with intent: because never for long, in reading Hardy, can we escape the accent of a young architect drawing up a specification, and sometimes all the Muses hold their ears in pain. Here he succeeded to no tradition: he was imperfectly educated, cramped by a book-language which he could not shake himself free of, and writing it with a stilted and self-conscious clumsiness. Much of his dialogue is composed in this strained falsetto: much of his narrative savours of the local reporter bent on doing justice to his theme. His errors are not those of an untrained taste, feeling towards a style which will not come. They are errors of practice in following unfortunate models — prose translations of the classics, for example — without perceiving their imperfection. And what is true of his style may be repeated of his craftmanship more generally: he never overcame his youthful addiction to melodrama: he never mastered the difference between strength and violence. Without the accompanying music of the pastoral theme, would *Tess* be tolerable?

V

With the publication of *Jude the Obscure* in 1895 Hardy, except for the slight fancy of *The Well-Beloved*, closed his career as a writer of prose fiction. His first volume of poems — many of them written at earlier dates — appeared three years later, when he was a man of fifty-eight. For the rest of his life, he wrote verse abundantly: the collected edition of his poems contains nearly a thousand pieces. In making my selection I have been guided by the wish to present, as truly as is possible within small compass, the poetic personality of the writer, and I have arranged it in conformity with the three aspects in which that personality most naturally presents itself to the reader. Hardy is as much a poet of place as Wordsworth or Cowper: but more than either of them he is a poet of local incident: of anecdote, tragic, humorous or cynical: of such drama as an earlier age might have cast into a ballad, or his own time into a novelette. But he is a poet of reflection also, of reflection on memory; and, taken together, his verses are, to a greater degree than is perhaps common with poets, a commentary, an old man's commentary on a life that had not been happy, nor, till its later years, much honoured with discipleship or public renown. Here he turns inward: and there is trouble in his eyes.

As a young man, bred on the border-line between rustic commerce and rustic gentility, he had been socially sensitive: susceptible to the charm of grace and breeding, and a little vexed with himself, perhaps, that he was so. He wished to raise himself: he thought of taking Orders, and the Rev. Thomas Hardy exchanging pulpits with the Rev. Leslie Stephen is one of the more piquant might-have-beens of history. Mill and Huxley barred the way: he abode by his profession of architect, and discharged his ambitions in a boyish work *The Poor Man and the Lady*, reminiscent, it would seem, at once of *Alton Locke* and *Maud*. His profession took him to Saint Juliot. And what happened there was what has happened and will happen from one generation to another. He fell in love with a girl with whom he was not intellectually in key. There was no open catastrophe: only the fire sank rapidly into vacancy and chill. But by some mysterious power Hardy was able to preserve, encysted as it were, this early passion in all its primal intensity; and so it came about that some of the most poignant love-poems in our language were written by an old man out of his memories of forty years before.

VI

A common accident befalling an uncommon man will work out its consequences in uncommon ways. And that Hardy was a man of endowments bestowed on few, *The Dynasts* exists to prove. Not long ago,

I had occasion to read it aloud all through, and at the end I thought : how far back must one go to find its match in power and beauty ? I paused for a while on *The Ring and the Book* : rather longer on *Don Juan*, and came to rest on the Third and Fourth Cantos of *Childe Harold*. Then other peaks showed through the mist : *Hyperion* and *Prometheus* ; the closing chorus of *Hellas* ; *Manfred* and *Cain*. It is from these heights, among the Titans who walk

> With Death and Morning on the silver horns,

that this poet, I thought, must be viewed and judged.

Titanism, or the spirit of revolt against an order felt to be unjust, first appears, I suppose, in English literature with Milton's Satan. Its strong recurrence in the early years of the last century is in large measure a political phenomenon, because an order which meant Sidmouth and Eldon at home, and the Holy Alliance abroad, was made to be revolted from. With the new Liberalism setting in victoriously after 1830, there was less call for an attitude which always edges perilously towards a mixture of self-pity and swelled head. But towards the middle of the century we see the spirit re-emerging quietly, gravely, ironically : defying nobody, denouncing nothing, simply disapproving.

> We, in some unknown Power's employ,
>   Move on a rigorous line ;
> Can neither when we will enjoy,
>   Nor, when we will, resign.

Both in thought and manner that is not very far removed from Hardy, though it was written when he

B   xvii

was a child of nine. And this of the same year is nearer still :

> Eat, drink and play, and think that this is bliss,
> There is no heaven but this,
>   There is no hell
> Save earth, which serves the purpose doubly well,
>   Seeing it visits still
> With equallest apportionment of ill
> Both good and bad alike, and brings to one same dust
> The unjust and the just.

That is how young men — Arnold's pupils — were thinking in 1849, ten years before the great storm broke.

If I were asked what the total effect of Darwin, Mill, Huxley, and Herbert Spencer upon their age had been, I should answer somehow thus. They made it difficult, almost to impossibility, for their younger contemporaries to retain the notion of a transcendent, governing Providence. They forced the imagination of their time into a monistic habit of thought, of which *The Dynasts* is the great, and solitary, artistic record. To those who pass that way, the various devices with which believers of another sort reconcile Providence with Evil, or with Pain, will almost necessarily seem servile or sophistical. For them, there is nothing to reconcile : because to them, inherent in It, in the essence and operation of It, abides

> the intolerable antilogy
> Of making figments feel.

The injustice of uncompensated pain, the darkening of our hours of happiness by the thought that

xviii

they too are passing towards Nothing, round these two themes Pessimism revolves in a closed circle. Men of an abundant, active temperament will not often think of them : men absorbed in some intellectual pursuit have little time to think of them. But for the meditative man there is no escape, and no consolation, except perhaps in constraining his temper to such an indifference as the ancient philosophies, Stoic and Epicurean, inculcated. And who can be sure that this equanimity will be proof against all shocks, from without, or from within ? Against pain, frustration, disappointment, wrong ?

VII

Hardy's pessimism is primarily that of the disappointed man, who cannot find the serenity which naturally attends on satisfaction and achievement, and feels himself ill-adjusted to an ill-adjusted world. It is the vast projection of an inner discord, untuning the music of the spheres. And as we follow his work forward from his early pastoral time we become aware that his growing preoccupation with one mode of this ill-adjustment, the disharmony of the Human Pair, is an artistic danger : that if he cannot keep it at the tragic height of *The Return*, it will slide into propaganda.

> The gods approve
> The depth and not the tumult of the soul :

and, as we go on, this tumult seems to be growing louder : there is a shrillness in the voice that pronounces doom, a helpless magnification of the personal discord : and we may feel that unless the Titan returns to his native peak, he will merit the graceless jibe about the Village Atheist brooding over the Village Idiot.

To his native peak ? Rather to his native vale.

" The choice," he wrote of *The Dynasts*, "the choice of such a subject was mainly due to three accidents of locality. It chanced that the writer was familiar with a part of England that lay within hail of the watering-place in which King George the Third had his favourite residence during the war with the first Napoleon, and where he was visited by ministers and others who bore the weight of English affairs on their more or less competent shoulders at that stressful time. Secondly, this district being also near the coast which had echoed with rumours of invasion in their intensest form while the descent threatened, was formerly animated by memories and traditions of the desperate military preparations for that contingency. Thirdly, the same countryside happened to be the birthplace of Nelson's flag captain at Trafalgar."

Thus it was from incidents of place that he conceived the inspiration of his drama. In place, and music, was his strength. As in Attic tragedy, however far the tale may range, still it is fixed to a few familiar points : here at Colonus the blind and exiled king found rest : here on the Areopagus the ways of God to man were justified : and the war-worn seamen in the camp at Troy think of Sunium, as, by the side of his dying Commander, the Flag Captain thinks

Thoughts all confused, my lord :— their needs on deck,
Your own sad state, and your unrivalled past ;
Mixed up with flashes of old things afar —
Old childish things at home, down Wessex way,
In the snug village under Blackdon Hill
Where I was born. The tumbling stream, the garden,
The placid look of the grey dial there,
Marking unconsciously this bloody hour,
And the red apples on my father's trees,
Just now full ripe.

VIII

But the theme, whatever its starting point, gave
him something which his own unaided imagination
could not provide. What Wordsworth said of
Goethe's poetry is true of Hardy's tragedy : it is not
inevitable enough. It is not in the nature of things
that Tess and Jude should come to their disastrous
ends. They are led there by a series of prepared
accidents for which their creator cannot convince
us that the Immanent Will, and not Thomas Hardy,
is responsible. If he is to persuade us that things
happen so, he must, like the Greek tragedians, take a
story where they did happen so, a real story, such
as the Woe of Thebes and the Curse of Atreus were
to those who saw them enacted on the stage.

The task, in fact, which Hardy set himself was to
create a form in which the busy variety of Shake-
spearean History should harmonise with the austere
and epic progress of an Aeschylean trilogy — its
two or three actors, its well-spaced incidents, its
long deliverances, its choric comment. "Readers
will readily discern," he said himself, "that The

Dynasts is intended simply for mental performance and not for the stage," and certainly he has left nothing undone to assist the reader's imagination, to keep it always at the right distance from the scene, and the scene always in focus. Here the professional exactitude of which I have spoken comes to his aid.

From high aloft, in the same July weather, and facing east, the vision swoops over the ocean and its coast-lines, from Cork Harbour on the extreme left, to Mondego Bay, Portugal, on the extreme right. Land's End and the Scilly Isles, Ushant and Cape Finisterre, are projecting features along the middle distance of the picture, and the English Channel recedes endwise as a tapering avenue near the centre.

DUMB SHOW

Four groups of moth-like transport ships are discovered silently skimming this wide liquid plain. The first group, to the right, is just vanishing behind Cape Mondego to enter Mondego Bay; the second, in the midst, has come out from Plymouth Sound, and is preparing to stand down Channel; the third is clearing St. Helen's point for the same course; and the fourth, much further up Channel, is obviously to follow on considerably in the rear of the two preceding. A south-east wind is blowing strong, and, according to the part of their course reached, they either sail direct with the wind on their larboard quarter, or labour forward by tacking in zigzags.

And he employs the same precision to bring forth " the unapparent," to penetrate through the " insistent substance," the atomies by which the drama must be enacted, to " the thing signified," the immeasurable, impersonal Thing which sustains it.

SPIRIT OF RUMOUR

It is a moment when the steadiest pulse
Thuds pit-a-pat. The crisis shapes and nears
For Wellington as for his counter-chief.

SPIRIT OF THE PITIES

The hour is shaking him, unshakeable
As he may seem !

SPIRIT OF THE YEARS

Know'st not at this stale time
That shaken and unshaken are alike
But demonstrations from the Back of Things?
Must I again reveal It as It hauls
The halyards of the world ?

A transparency as in earlier scenes again pervades the spectacle, and the ubiquitous urging of the Immanent Will becomes visualized. The web connecting all the apparently separate shapes includes WELLINGTON in its tissue with the rest, and shows him, like them, as acting while discovering his intention to act. By the lurid light the faces of every row, square, group, and column of men, French and English, wear the expression of people in a dream.

SPIRIT OF THE PITIES (*tremulously*)
Yea, Sire ; I see.
Disquiet me, pray, no more !

The strange light passes, and the embattled hosts on the field seem to move independently as usual.

The result is that nowhere are we conscious of any unreality, or any hollow place. The whole piece, apparent and unapparent, is compact, coherent and convincing. Given the initial surrender of the imagination which every work of art requires, this, we feel, in the world here displayed, is how things must happen.

IX

And what is this world ? It is the same with that of the Tramp Woman, and the ill-motherings of Pydel Vale — perhaps Hardy's most tragic ballad — and a hundred personal pieces. It is a world of almost unimaginable contrasts, not reducible, yet, to any satisfying synthesis : and of these the greatest, the most insistent, the most oppressive, is the disproportion between the effort of the individual, his aspirations and intentions, his capacity for good or evil, joy or pain, and the silent impersonality of that Universe out of which he is mysteriously projected into a short consciousness, by which for a brief while he is sustained, and into which he is again and for ever absorbed. But Hardy has in many places expressly disclaimed both the pretensions of a philosopher and the name of pessimist. "My alleged pessimism," he wrote in the Preface to *Late Lyrics and Earlier*, "is in truth only ' questionings ' in the exploration of reality, and is the first step towards the soul's betterment, and the body's also." Not indeed that even from this betterment much is to be hoped : only " that pain to all upon the earth, tongued or dumb, shall be kept down to a minimum by loving-kindness, operating through scientific knowledge, and actuated by the modicum of free-will conjecturally possessed by organic life when the mighty necessitating forces — unconscious or other — that have ' the balancing of the clouds ',

xxiv

happen to be in equilibrium, which may or may not be often." His pessimism, in other words, is not to be read as despair, but as a resigned waiting on events which he will never see, and which very likely will never come to pass : especially on one event, transcending and transforming all the others, which he contemplates with wistful speculation : on the emergence of consciousness, or loving-kindness — his favourite word — in the necessitating forces themselves.

X

I have spoken of Hardy's lyrics as a commentary on his own life, a commentary redeemed from egoism by its obvious and intense sincerity, and rarely, if ever, sounding that note of self-pity which is so persistent in much Victorian poetry. But among them there is a group, *In Tenebris*, written about 1895, which I have not included in my selection but reserved for this place, because it seems to me to be an interpretation of the commentary, and to place Hardy, more exactly than anything else he has left, in relation to his contemporaries, and to the movement of poetic thought in his time.

They open with a slow movement in a minor key.

IN TENEBRIS

I

" Percussus sum sicut foenum, et aruit cor meum."—Ps. **ci.**

Wintertime nighs ;
But my bereavement-pain
It cannot bring again :
Twice no one dies.

Flower-petals flee ;
But, since it once hath been,
No more that severing scene
    Can harrow me.

Birds faint in dread :
I shall not lose old strength
In the lone frost's black length :
    Strength long since fled !

Leaves freeze to dun ;
But friends can not turn cold
This season as of old
    For him with none.

Tempests may scath ;
But love can not make smart
Again this year his heart
    Who no heart hath.

Black is night's cope ;
But death will not appal
One who, past doubtings all,
    Waits in unhope.

Much might be said of these few stanzas only. I will only note : the simplicity of their metrical structure, the perfect carrying-through of the stated theme ; contrasted with this, the awkwardness in places of the diction, the obstinate choice — as it seems, for careless it is not — of the lifeless word

No more that severing scene
    Can *harrow* me :

and the quality of the vision disclosed in the line

In the lone frost's *black* length.

With the gift, so widely diffused in the Victorian age, the power of bringing word and image together in one movement of the mind, Hardy was not abundantly endowed. Now and then his observation flowers into a sudden and exquisite perception as in the magnificent epithet

O the opal and the sapphire of that *wandering* western sea.

But for the most part his landscape is thought out, and must be thought again by the reader before the reader sees it, as he does not need to think when Tennyson, for example, takes up the poetic brush. "The lone frost's black length" is not a direct picture: it is, for all its brevity, a composition, and will hardly, perhaps, convey its full meaning till it has recalled the vivid blackness of hedge and covert seen against the snow.

In the second movement Hardy shifts, with a satirical intent which the metre at once discloses, to the high-spirited recitation-couplets of popular poetry.

" Considerabam ad dexteram, et videbam ; et non erat qui cognosceret me. . . . Non est qui requirat animam meam."—Ps. cxli.

When the clouds' swoln bosoms echo back the shouts of the
    many and strong
That things are all as they best may be, save a few to be right
    ere long,
And my eyes have not the vision in them to discern what to
    these is so clear,
The blot seems straightway in me alone ; one better he were
    not here.

The stout upstanders say, All's well with us : ruers have
    nought to ruc !
And what the potent say so oft, can it fail to be somewhat
    true ?

Breezily go they, breezily come ; their dust smokes around
    their career,
Till I think I am one born out of due time, who has no calling
    here.

Their dawns bring lusty joys, it seems ; their evenings all
    that is sweet ;
Our times are blessed times, they cry : Life shapes it as is
    most meet,
And nothing is much the matter ; there are many smiles to a
    tear ;
Then what is the matter is I, I say. Why should such an one
    be here ? . . .

Let him in whose ears the low-voiced Best is killed by the
    clash of the First,
Who holds that if way to the Better there be, it exacts a full
    look at the Worst,
Who feels that delight is a delicate growth cramped by
    crookedness, custom, and fear,
Get him up and be gone as one shaped awry ; he disturbs the
    order here.

So much for Robert Browning, and Rabbi Ben Ezra,
and all who never doubt that clouds will break !
    Near the end of his life he chose that line

Who holds that if way to the Better there be, it exacts a full
    look at the Worst,

as the watchword of his " questionings " : and
perhaps the line before it hints at the secret of his
private trouble. It does not matter : a child's sorrow
over a dead bird can be as keen as a man's over a
broken life, and remembered as long. The trouble
was there, and it was not to be put by. Like his age,

Hardy was growing tired: tired of compromise and conventions: of customs and conformities: but only in passive revolt. Still, now and then a note sounds, surely recalling an older voice, and the rebel of an earlier age. For three hundred years, as I have said elsewhere, what may be called our poetic attitude to the world was in the main Spenserian, and to Spenser, Donne, in his intellectualism and his rejection of the romantic lure, is the obvious antithesis. But not more obvious than Hardy. How Hardy might have written had he been born an Elizabethan, it is amusing to conjecture, if impossible to say. But how Donne might have written if he had been a younger contemporary of Meredith it is easier at least to guess.

> Yes ; we'll wed, my little fay,
>   And you shall write you mine,
> And in a villa chastely gray
>   We'll house, and sleep, and dine.
>   But those night-screened, divine,
>   Stolen trysts of heretofore,
> We of choice ecstasies and fine
>   Shall know no more.
>
> The formal faced cohue
>   Will then no more upbraid
> With smiting smiles and whisperings two
>   Who have thrown less loves in shade.
>   We shall no more evade
>   The searching light of the sun,
> Our game of passion will be played,
>   Our dreaming done.

But what to an Elizabethan could only be a turbulence of the spirit, to be atoned for at the right time by a passionate repentance, was to a Victorian, to a man living under the new cosmogony disclosed by science, no turbulence but a profound questioning and one that went down to the very roots of life, the springs of destiny. It is always the same contrast, but this time in its most intimate, haunting form : the vast power of Nature to create, and the impoverished, strained, conventional material which our social discipline has made for Nature to work on. It was the riddle of his day : not to be solved, only to be felt : only to be endured : in rare bright hours perhaps to be forgotten, and to be remembered the more keenly for that brief oblivion.

" Heu mihi, quia incolatus meus prolongatus est ! Habitavi cum habitantibus Cedar ; multum incola fuit anima mea."—Ps. cxx.

There have been times when I well might have passed and the
    ending have come —
Points in my path when the dark might have stolen on me,
    artless, unrueing —
Ere I had learnt that the world was a welter of futile doing ;
Such had been times when I well might have passed, and the
    ending have come !

Say, on the noon when the half-sunny hours told that April
    was nigh,
And I upgathered and cast forth the snow from the crocus-
    border,
Fashioned and furbished the soil into a summer-seeming order,
Glowing in gladsome faith that I quickened the year thereby.

Or on that loneliest of eves when afar and benighted we stood,
She who upheld me and I, in the midmost of Egdon together,

Confident I in her watching and ward through the blackening
    heather,
Deeming her matchless in might and with measureless scope
    endued.

Or on that winter-wild night when, reclined by the chimney-
    nook quoin,
Slowly a drowse overgat me, the smallest and feeblest of folk
    there,
Weak from my baptism of pain ; when at times and anon I
    awoke there —
Heard of a world wheeling on, with no listing or longing to
    join.

Even then I while unweeting that vision could vex or that
    knowledge could numb,
That sweets to the mouth in the belly are bitter, and tart, and
    untoward,
Then, on some dim-coloured scene should my briefly raised
    curtain have lowered,
Then might the Voice that is law have said "Cease!" and the
    ending have come.

But it does not come.

XI

Hardy was of no school and he created none.
From the great procession of nineteenth-century
poetry he stands aloof, a lonely figure, always
observant, not ready of speech : rooted in his native
soil, and responsive to every passing warmth, or
bitterness, in the air ; shrinking and stubborn,
compassionate and austere. Here we shall not find
the romantic gusto of Meredith or Browning, or the
classic graces of Arnold and Tennyson ; or the

joyous energy with which William Morris created his happily ordered world. Often in reading Hardy, especially in reading the muted blank verse of *The Dynasts*, I have recalled the words in which he describes the Christmas mummers of his childhood, and "the curiously hypnotizing impressiveness of their automatic style, that of persons who spoke by no will of their own." At the end, it is to the simplicity, the unpretentious integrity, of Hardy's verse that those who have once caught the note find themselves returning. His poetry is all of a piece, the utterance, often harsh, often casual, of a mind that knows itself, that is content with no derived philosophy, seeing things as it must see them and speaking about them as it must speak. His style has not the natural grandeur of Wordsworth, to name the poet with whom his meditative habit of mind most closely associates him. Rather, its characterizing note is a certain impersonal dignity, such as we may still often find, in company with a surface clumsiness of manner and a tongue-tied difficulty of speech, in men of Hardy's country and Hardy's stock.

The wind bloweth where it listeth, and the spirit of the age may choose to speak, now in the accent of a rebel prince, as it did when Byron filled Europe with his voice, and now in the tone of an ageing man watching the fire die down, and thinking of old tunes, old memories : moments remembered at railway stations and lodging-houses ; sunsets at the end of London streets, water coming over the weir, the rain on the downs. But what we hear is the voice of an age, of a generation carried beyond sight of its old landmarks, and gazing doubtfully down an illimitable vista, of cosmic changes endlessly proceeding, and ephemeral suffering endlessly to be renewed. Twilight was coming on: an evening chill was in the air.

Of that chill, that twilight, and all its memories of noontide gone, Hardy is the poet. But his stature is not to be measured only by his aptness to the mood of his time. More is needed of a poet than that he should say acceptably what his own generation is most ready to hear, though that, doubtless, is needed too, if his voice is to be heard; and among the accomplished versifiers of his later time Hardy was listened to with respect rather than acclaim, and with little of such regard as incites to imitation. Nor is it enough that a poet should record for future ages the life and landscape of his day, as Shakespeare has preserved the shearing feasts of Cotswold, or Virgil the Italian scene, unless like them he has the art to make the record a thing of poetic price itself. Beside this, what the world asks of its poets and what it remembers them by, is a certain mastery, as we may say, of the meaning of their time, and a certain power to bring this meaning — thought, and feeling about thought, and reflection upon feeling — home to other ages.

The volcanic inroads made by science and invention upon the ancient fields of life and belief in Europe were, with us, for a long time masked, and partly concealed, by the tenacity with which we clung to our traditional institutions, the vigour with which we defended them from imminent, inevitable change; the attachment they inspired. We misread the Victorian age if we do not apprehend how deep, how intimate and how sincere were the feelings that gathered round, and sustained, its customary life, its religion and its domestic order. But a time will always come when custom, no longer needed as a defence against precipitate innovation, becomes a burden and an impediment. The adjustment is no long instinctive but deliberate, and, being deliberate, brings with it a sense of uneasiness, of weariness, of resentment. And of all this Hardy is the poet too. This is what the Late Victorian age meant, this is what it stands for in the history of the English mind — here we see with what presuppositions men of a good intelligence thought, what themes engaged their minds and stirred their sympathies, by what canons they judged of things : the pressure of custom, the breaking up of custom, the anxious view into a world where custom had dissolved : the craving, no longer for certitude of mind — that dream has gone — but for serenity of soul, not sovereign over circumstance, but at least in harmony with itself. And there we may leave the poet as the darkness gathers about him and his world, wistfully speculating on an alliance, by means of "the inter-fusing effect of poetry," between "religion, which must be retained unless the world is to perish," and "complete rationality," without which the world will also perish, and, for the last time, circling home to the place from which he had come, to the prayers, the music, and the very stones of the village church.

G. M. YOUNG.

OARE, 1940.

POEMS OF PLACE AND INCIDENT

A TRAMPWOMAN'S TRAGEDY

(182–)

I

FROM Wynyard's Gap the livelong day,
  The livelong day,
We beat afoot the northward way
  We had travelled times before.
The sun-blaze burning on our backs,
Our shoulders sticking to our packs,
By fosseway, fields, and turnpike tracks
  We skirted sad Sedge-Moor.

II

Full twenty miles we jaunted on,
  We jaunted on, —
My fancy-man, and jeering John,
  And Mother Lee, and I.
And, as the sun drew down to west,
We climbed the toilsome Poldon crest,
And saw, of landskip sights the best,
  The inn that beamed thereby.

III

For months we had padded side by side,
  Ay, side by side
Through the Great Forest, Blackmoor wide,
  And where the Parret ran.
We'd faced the gusts on Mendip ridge,
Had crossed the Yeo unhelped by bridge,
Been stung by every Marshwood midge,
  I and my fancy-man.

3

IV

Lone inns we loved, my man and I,
  My man and I ;
" King's Stag," " Windwhistle " high and dry,
  " The Horse " on Hintock Green,
The cosy house at Wynyard's Gap,
" The Hut " renowned on Bredy Knap,
And many another wayside tap
  Where folk might sit unseen.

V

Now as we trudged — O deadly day
  O deadly day ! —
I teased my fancy-man in play
  And wanton idleness.
I walked alongside jeering John,
I laid his hand my waist upon ;
I would not bend my glances on
  My lover's dark distress.

VI

Thus Poldon top at last we won,
  At last we won,
And gained the inn at sink of sun
  Far-famed as " Marshal's Elm."
Beneath us figured tor and lea,
From Mendip to the western sea —
I doubt if finer sight there be
  Within this royal realm.

Inside the settle all a-row —
    All four a-row
We sat, I next to John, to show
    That he had wooed and won.
And then he took me on his knee,
And swore it was his turn to be
My favoured mate, and Mother Lee
    Passed to my former one.

Then in a voice I had never heard,
    I had never heard,
My only Love to me : " One word,
    My lady, if you please !
Whose is the child you are like to bear ? —
His ? After all my months o' care ? "
God knows 'twas not ! But, O despair !
    I nodded — still to tease.

Then up he sprung, and with his knife —
    And with his knife
He let out jeering Johnny's life,
    Yes ; there, at set of sun.
The slant ray through the window nigh
Gilded John's blood and glazing eye,
Ere scarcely Mother Lee and I
    Knew that the deed was done.

The taverns tell the gloomy tale,
    The gloomy tale,
How that at Ivel-chester jail
    My Love, my sweetheart swung ;
Though stained till now by no misdeed
Save one horse ta'en in time o' need ;
(Blue Jimmy stole right many a steed
    Ere his last fling he flung.)

XI

Thereaft I walked the world alone,
    Alone, alone !
On his death-day I gave my groan
    And dropt his dead-born child.
'Twas nigh the jail, beneath a tree,
None tending me ; for Mother Lee
Had died at Glaston, leaving me
    Unfriended on the wild.

XII

And in the night as I lay weak,
    As I lay weak,
The leaves a-falling on my cheek,
    The red moon low declined —
The ghost of him I'd die to kiss
Rose up and said : " Ah, tell me this !
Was the child mine, or was it his ?
    Speak, that I rest may find ! "

XIII

O doubt not but I told him then,
    I told him then,
That I had kept me from all men
    Since we joined lips and swore.
Whereat he smiled, and thinned away
As the wind stirred to call up day . . .
— 'Tis past ! And here alone I stray
    Haunting the Western Moor.

NOTES. — "Windwhistle" (Stanza iv). The highness and
dryness of Windwhistle Inn was impressed upon the writer
two or three years ago, when, after climbing on a hot afternoon
to the beautiful spot near which it stands and entering the inn
for tea, he was informed by the landlady that none could be
had, unless he would fetch water from a valley half a mile off,
the house containing not a drop, owing to its situation. However, a tantalizing row of full barrels behind her back testified
to a wetness of a certain sort, which was not at that time desired.

"Marshal's Elm" (Stanza vi), so picturesquely situated, is no
longer an inn, though the house, or part of it, still remains. It
used to exhibit a fine old swinging sign.

"Blue Jimmy" (Stanza x) was a notorious horse-stealer of
Wessex in those days, who appropriated more than a hundred
horses before he was caught, among others one belonging to a
neighbour of the writer's grandfather. He was hanged at the
now demolished Ivel-chester or Ilchester jail above mentioned
— that building formerly of so many sinister associations in the
minds of the local peasantry, and the continual haunt of fever,
which at last led to its condemnation. Its site is now an
innocent-looking green meadow.

A SUNDAY MORNING TRAGEDY

(*circa* 186-)

I BORE a daughter flower-fair,
In Pydel Vale, alas for me ;
I joyed to mother one so rare,
But dead and gone I now would be.

Men looked and loved her as she grew,
And she was won, alas for me ;
She told me nothing, but I knew,
And saw that sorrow was to be.

I knew that one had made her thrall,
A thrall to him, alas for me ;
And then, at last, she told me all,
And wondered what her end would be.

She owned that she had loved too well,
Had loved too well, unhappy she,
And bore a secret time would tell,
Though in her shroud she'd sooner be.

I plodded to her sweetheart's door
In Pydel Vale, alas for me :
I pleaded with him, pleaded sore,
To save her from her misery.

He frowned, and swore he could not wed,
Seven times he swore it could not be ;
"Poverty's worse than shame," he said,
Till all my hope went out of me.

"I've packed my traps to sail the main" —
Roughly he spake, alas did he —
"Wessex beholds me not again,
'Tis worse than any jail would be!"

— There was a shepherd whom I knew
A subtle man, alas for me:
I sought him all the pastures through,
Though better I had ceased to be.

I traced him by his lantern light,
And gave him hint, alas for me,
Of how she found her in the plight
That is so scorned in Christendie.

"Is there an herb. . . . ?" I asked. "Or none?"
Yes, thus I asked him desperately.
"— There is," he said; "a certain one. . . ."
Would he had sworn that none knew he!

"To-morrow I will walk your way,"
He hinted low, alas for me. —
Fieldwards I gazed throughout next day;
Now fields I never more would see!

The sunset-shine, as curfew strook,
As curfew strook beyond the lea,
Lit his white smock and gleaming crook,
While slowly he drew near to me.

He pulled from underneath his smock
The herb I sought, my curse to be —
"At times I use it in my flock,"
He said, and hope waxed strong in me.

" 'Tis meant to balk ill-motherings " —
(Ill-motherings ! Why should they be ?) —
" If not, would God have sent such things ? "
So spoke the shepherd unto me.

That night I watched the poppling brew,
With bended back and hand on knee :
I stirred it till the dawnlight grew,
And the wind whiffled wailfully.

" This scandal shall be slain," said I,
" That lours upon her innocency :
I'll give all whispering tongues the lie ; " —
But worse than whispers was to be.

" Here's physic for untimely fruit,"
I said to her, alas for me,
Early that morn in fond salute ;
And in my grave I now would be.

— Next Sunday came, with sweet church chimes
In Pydel Vale, alas for me :
I went into her room betimes ;
No more may such a Sunday be !

" Mother, instead of rescue nigh,"
She faintly breathed, alas for me,
" I feel as I were like to die,
And underground soon, soon should be."

From church that noon the people walked
In twos and threes, alas for me,
Showed their new raiment — smiled and talked,
Though sackcloth-clad I longed to be.

10

Came to my door her lover's friends,
And cheerly cried, alas for me,
" Right glad are we he makes amends,
For never a sweeter bride can be."

My mouth dried, as 'twere scorched within,
Dried at their words, alas for me :
More and more neighbours crowded in,
(O why should mothers ever be !)

" Ha-ha !   Such well-kept news ! " laughed they,
Yes — so they laughed, alas for me.
" Whose banns were called in church to-day ? " —
Christ, how I wished my soul could flee !

" Where is she ?   O the stealthy miss,"
Still bantered they, alas for me,
" To keep a wedding close as this. . . ."
Ay, Fortune worked thus wantonly !

" But you are pale — you did not know ? "
They archly asked, alas for me.
I stammered, " Yes — some days — ago,"
While coffined clay I wished to be.

" 'Twas done to please her, we surmise ? "
(They spoke quite lightly in their glee)
" Done by him as a fond surprise ? "
I thought their words would madden me.

Her lover entered.   " Where's my bird ? —
My bird — my flower — my picotee ?
First time of asking, soon the third ! "
Ah, in my grave I well may be.

To me he whispered : " Since your call — "
So spoke he then, alas for me —
" I've felt for her, and righted all."
— I think of it to agony.

" She's faint to-day — tired — nothing more — "
Thus did I lie, alas for me. . . .
I called her at her chamber door
As one who scarce had strength to be.

No voice replied. I went within —
O women ! scourged the worst are we. . . .
I shrieked. The others hastened in
And saw the stroke there dealt on me.

There she lay — silent, breathless, dead,
Stone dead she lay — wronged, sinless she ! —
Ghost-white the cheeks once rosy-red :
Death had took her. Death took not me.

I kissed her colding face and hair,
I kissed her corpse — the bride to be ! —
My punishment I cannot bear,
But pray God *not* to pity me.

THE RASH BRIDE

An Experience of the Mellstock Quire

I

We Christmas-carolled down the Vale, and up the
    Vale, and round the Vale,
We played and sang that night as we were yearly
    wont to do —
A carol in a minor key, a carol in the major D,
Then at each house : " Good wishes : many
    Christmas joys to you ! "

II

Next, to the widow's John and I and all the rest
    drew on.   And I
Discerned that John could hardly hold the tongue
    of him for joy.
The widow was a sweet young thing whom John
    was bent on marrying,
And quiring at her casement seemed romantic to
    the boy.

III

" She'll make reply, I trust," said he, " to our
    salute ?   She must ! " said he,
" And then I will accost her gently — much to her
    surprise ! —
For knowing not I am with you here, when I speak
    up and call her dear
A tenderness will fill her voice, a bashfulness her
    eyes."

13

So, by her window-square we stood; ay, with our
    lanterns there we stood,
And he along with us, — not singing, waiting for
    a sign;
And when we'd quired her carols three a light was
    lit and out looked she,
A shawl about her bedgown, and her colour red as
    wine.

V

And sweetly then she bowed her thanks, and
    smiled, and spoke aloud her thanks;
When lo, behind her back there, in the room, a man
    appeared.
I knew him — one from Woolcomb way — Giles
    Swetman — honest as the day,
But eager, hasty; and I felt that some strange
    trouble neared.

VI

" How comes he there? . . . Suppose," said we,
    " she's wed of late! Who knows? " said we.
— " She married yester-morning — only mother yet
    has known
The secret o't! " shrilled one small boy. "But now
    I've told, let's wish 'em joy! "
A heavy fall aroused us: John had gone down like
    a stone.

VII

We rushed to him and caught him round, and lifted
    him, and brought him round,

When, hearing something wrong had happened,
    oped the window she :
" Has one of you fallen ill ? " she asked, " by these
    night labours overtasked ? "
None answered. That she'd done poor John a cruel
    turn felt we.

VIII

Till up spoke Michael : " Fie, young dame !
    You've broke your promise, sly young dame,
By forming this new tie, young dame, and jilting
    John so true,
Who trudged to-night to sing to 'ee because he
    thought he'd bring to 'ee
Good wishes as your coming spouse. May ye such
    trifling rue ! "

IX

Her man had said no word at all ; but being behind
    had heard it all,
And now cried : " Neighbours, on my soul I knew
    not 'twas like this ! "
And then to her : " If I had known you'd had in tow
    not me alone,
No wife should you have been of mine. It is a dear-
    bought bliss ! "

X

She changed death-white, and heaved a cry : we'd
    never heard so grieved a cry
As came from her at this from him : heartbroken
    quite seemed she ;

D

And suddenly, as we looked on, she turned, and
    rushed ; and she was gone,
Whither, her husband, following after, knew not ;
    nor knew we.

XI

We searched till dawn about the house ; within the
    house, without the house,
We searched among the laurel boughs that grew
    beneath the wall,
And then among the crocks and things, and stores
    for winter junketings,
In linhay, loft, and dairy ; but we found her not
    at all.

XII

Then John rushed in : " O friends," he said, " hear
    this, this, this ! " and bends his head :
" I've — searched round by the — *well*, and find the
    cover open wide !
I am fearful that — I can't say what . . . Bring
    lanterns, and some cords to knot."
We did so, and we went and stood the deep dark
    hole beside.

XIII

And then they, ropes in hand, and I — ay, John,
    and all the band, and I
Let down a lantern to the depths — some hundred
    feet and more ;
It glimmered like a fog-dimmed star ; and there,
    beside its light, afar,
White drapery floated, and we knew the meaning
    that it bore.

XIV

The rest is naught. . . . We buried her o' Sunday.
    Neighbours carried her ;
And Swetman — he who'd married her — now
    miserablest of men,
Walked mourning first ; and then walked John ;
    just quivering, but composed anon ;
And we the quire formed round the grave, as was
    the custom then.

XV

Our old bass player, as I recall — his white hair
    blown — but why recall ! —
His viol upstrapped, bent figure — doomed to
    follow her full soon —
Stood bowing, pale and tremulous ; and next to
    him the rest of us. . . .
We sang the Ninetieth Psalm to her — set to Saint
    Stephen's tune.

THE HOMECOMING

GRUFFLY growled the wind on Toller downland broad and
    bare,
And lonesome was the house, and dark ; and few came
    there.

" Now don't ye rub your eyes so red ; we're home
    and have no cares ;
Here's a skimmer-cake for supper, peckled onions,
    and some pears ;
I've got a little keg o' summat strong, too, under
    stairs :
— What, slight your husband's victuals ? Other
    brides can tackle theirs ! "

The wind of winter mooed and mouthed their chimney like
    a horn,
And round the house and past the house 'twas leafless and
    lorn.

" But my dear and tender poppet, then, how came
    ye to agree
In Ivel church this morning ? Sure, there-right you
    married me ! "
— " Hoo-hoo ! — I don't know — I forgot how
    strange and far 'twould be,
An' I wish I was at home again with dear daddee ! "

Gruffly growled the wind on Toller downland broad and
    bare,
And lonesome was the house, and dark ; and few came
    there.

" I didn't think such furniture as this was all you'd
    own,
And great black beams for ceiling, and a floor o'
    wretched stone,
And nasty pewter platters, horrid forks of steel and
    bone,
And a monstrous crock in chimney. 'Twas to me
    quite unbeknown ! "

Rattle went the door ; down flapped a cloud of smoke,
As shifting north the wicked wind assayed a smarter stroke.

" Now sit ye by the fire, poppet ; put yourself at
    ease :
And keep your little thumb out of your mouth,
    dear, please !
And I'll sing to 'ee a pretty song of lovely flowers
    and bees,
And happy lovers taking walks within a grove o'
    trees."

Gruffly growled the wind on Toller Down, so bleak and
    bare,
And lonesome was the house, and dark ; and few came
    there.

" Now, don't ye gnaw your handkercher ; 'twill
    hurt your little tongue,
And if you do feel spitish, 'tis because ye are over
    young ;
But you'll be getting older, like us all, ere very long,
And you'll see me as I am — a man who never did
    'ee wrong."

Straight from Whit'sheet Hill to Benvill Lane the
*   blusters pass,*
Hitting hedges, milestones, handposts, trees, and tufts of
*   grass.*

" Well, had I only known, my dear, that this was
        how you'd be,
I'd have married her of riper years that was so fond
        of me.
But since I can't, I've half a mind to run away to
        sea,
And leave 'ee to go barefoot to your d—d
        daddee ! "

Up one wall and down the other — past each window-
*   pane —*
Prance the gusts, and then away down Crimmercrock's
*   long lane.*

" I — I — don't know what to say to't, since your
        wife I've vowed to be ;
And as 'tis done, I s'pose here I must bide — poor
        me !
Aye — as you are ki-ki-kind, I'll try to live along
        with 'ee,
Although I'd fain have stayed at home with dear
        daddee ! "

Gruffly growled the wind on Toller Down, so bleak and
*   bare,*
And lonesome was the house, and dark ; and few came
*   there.*

" That's right, my Heart !   And though on haunted
     Toller Down we be,
And the wind swears things in chimley, we'll to
     supper merrily !
So don't ye tap your shoe so pettish-like ; but smile
     at me,
And ye'll soon forget to sock and sigh for dear
     daddee ! "

THE CURATE'S KINDNESS

A Workhouse Irony

I

I THOUGHT they'd be strangers aroun' me,
    But she's to be there !
Let me jump out o' waggon and go back and
        drown me
    At Pummery or Ten-Hatches Weir.

II

I thought : " Well, I've come to the Union —
    The workhouse at last —
After honest hard work all the week, and
        Communion
    O' Zundays, these fifty years past.

III

" 'Tis hard ; but," I thought, " never mind it :
    There's gain in the end :
And when I get used to the place I shall find it
    A home, and may find there a friend.

IV

" Life there will be better than t'other,
    For peace is assured.
The men in one wing and their wives in another
    Is strictly the rule of the Board."

Just then one young Pa'son arriving
    Steps up out of breath
To the side o' the waggon wherein we were driving
    To Union ; and calls out and saith :   .

VI

" Old folks, that harsh order is altered,
    Be not sick of heart !
The Guardians they poohed and they pished and
      they paltered
    When urged not to keep you apart.

VII

" ' It is wrong,' I maintained, ' to divide them,
    Near forty years wed.'
' Very well, sir. We promise, then, they shall abide
      them
    In one wing together,' they said."

VIII

Then I sank — knew 'twas quite a foredone thing
    That misery should be
To the end ! . . . To get freed of her there was the
      one thing
    Had made the change welcome to me.

IX

To go there was ending but badly ;
    'Twas shame and 'twas pain ;

"But anyhow," thought I, "thereby I shall gladly
    Get free of this forty years' chain."

x

I thought they'd be strangers aroun' me,
    But she's to be there!
Let me jump out o' waggon and go back and
      drown me
    At Pummery or Ten-Hatches Weir.

AFTER THE CLUB-DANCE

BLACK'ON frowns east on Maidon,
   And westward to the sea,
But on neither is his frown laden
   With scorn, as his frown on me !

At dawn my heart grew heavy,
   I could not sip the wine,
I left the jocund bevy
   And that young man o' mine.

The roadside elms pass by me, —
   Why do I sink with shame
When the birds a-perch there eye me ?
   They, too, have done the same !

A CHURCH ROMANCE

(Mellstock : *circa* 1835)

SHE turned in the high pew, until her sight
Swept the west gallery, and caught its row
Of music-men with viol, book, and bow
Against the sinking sad tower-window light.

She turned again ; and in her pride's despite
One strenuous viol's inspirer seemed to throw
A message from his string to her below,
Which said : " I claim thee as my own forthright ! "

Thus their hearts' bond began, in due time signed.
And long years thence, when Age had scared
    Romance,
At some old attitude of his or glance
That gallery-scene would break upon her mind,
With him as minstrel, ardent, young, and trim,
Bowing " New Sabbath " or " Mount Ephraim."

THE STRANGER'S SONG

(As sung by Mr. Charles Charrington in the play of
" The Three Wayfarers ")

O MY trade it is the rarest one,
     Simple shepherds all —
  My trade is a sight to see ;
For my customers I tie, and take 'em up on high,
  And waft 'em to a far countree !

My tools are but common ones,
     Simple shepherds all —
  My tools are no sight to see :
A little hempen string, and a post whereon to swing,
  Are implements enough for me !

To-morrow is my working day,
     Simple shepherds all —
  To-morrow is a working day for me :
For the farmer's sheep is slain, and the lad who did
    it ta'en,
  And on his soul may God ha' mer-cy !

THE OXEN

CHRISTMAS EVE, and twelve of the clock.
  " Now they are all on their knees,"
An elder said as we sat in a flock
  By the embers in hearthside ease.

We pictured the meek mild creatures where
  They dwelt in their strawy pen,
Nor did it occur to one of us there
  To doubt they were kneeling then.

So fair a fancy few would weave
  In these years ! Yet, I feel,
If someone said on Christmas Eve,
  " Come ; see the oxen kneel

" In the lonely barton by yonder coomb
  Our childhood used to know,"
I should go with him in the gloom,
  Hoping it might be so.

  1915

THE FALLOW DEER AT THE LONELY HOUSE

ONE without looks in to-night
    Through the curtain-chink
From the sheet of glistening white;
One without looks in to-night
    As we sit and think
    By the fender-brink.

We do not discern those eyes
    Watching in the snow;
Lit by lamps of rosy dyes
We do not discern those eyes
    Wondering, aglow,
    Fourfooted, tiptoe.

THE MILESTONE BY THE RABBIT-BURROW

(On Yell'ham Hill)

In my loamy nook
As I dig my hole
I observe men look
At a stone, and sigh
As they pass it by
To some far goal.

Something it says
To their glancing eyes
That must distress
The frail and lame,
And the strong of frame
Gladden or surprise.

Do signs on its face
Declare how far
Feet have to trace
Before they gain
Some blest champaign
Where no gins are?

" ALIVE ? " — And I leapt in my wonder,
  Was faint of my joyance,
And grasses and grove shone in garments
  Of glory to me.

" She lives, in a plenteous well-being,
  To-day as aforehand ;
The dead bore the name — though a rare one —
  The name that bore she."

She lived . . . I, afar in the city
  Of frenzy-led factions,
Had squandered green years and maturer
  In bowing the knee

To Baals illusive and specious,
  Till chance had there voiced me
That one I loved vainly in nonage
  Had ceased her to be.

The passion the planets had scowled on,
  And change had let dwindle,
Her death-rumour smartly relifted
  To full apogee.

I mounted a steed in the dawning
  With acheful remembrance,
And made for the ancient West Highway
  To far Exonb'ry.

Passing heaths, and the House of Long Sieging,
   I neared the thin steeple
That tops the fair fane of Poore's olden
   Episcopal see ;

And, changing anew my blown bearer,
   I traversed the downland
Whereon the bleak hill-graves of Chieftains
   Bulge barren of tree ;

And still sadly onward I followed
   That Highway the Icen,
Which trails its pale riband down Wessex
   By lynchet and lea.

Along through the Stour-bordered Forum,
   Where Legions had wayfared,
And where the slow river-face glasses
   Its green canopy,

And by Weatherbury Castle, and thencefrom
   Through Casterbridge held I
Still on, to entomb her my mindsight
   Saw stretched pallidly.

No highwayman's trot blew the night-wind
   To me so life-weary,
But only the creak of a gibbet
   Or waggoner's jee.

Triple-ramparted Maidon gloomed grayly
   Above me from southward,
And north the hill-fortress of Eggar
   And square Pummerie.

The Nine-Pillared Cromlech, the Bride-streams,
    The Axe, and the Otter
I passed, to the gate of the city
    Where Exe scents the sea;

Till, spent, in the graveacre pausing,
    I learnt 'twas not *my* Love
To whom Mother Church had just murmured
    A last lullaby.

— "Then, where dwells the Canon's kinswoman,
    My friend of aforetime?"
I asked, to disguise my heart-heavings
    And new ecstasy.

"She wedded." — "Ah!" — "Wedded beneath
    her —
    She keeps the stage-hostel
Ten miles hence, beside the great Highway —
    The famed Lions-Three.

"Her spouse was her lackey — no option
    'Twixt wedlock and worse things;
A lapse over-sad for a lady
    Of her pedigree!"

I shuddered, said nothing, and wandered
    To shades of green laurel:
More ghastly than death were these tidings
    Of life's irony!

For, on my ride down I had halted
    Awhile at the Lions,

And her — her whose name had once opened
    My heart as a key —

I'd looked on, unknowing, and witnessed
    Her jests with the tapsters,
Her liquor-fired face, her thick accents
    In naming her fee.

" O God, why this seeming derision ! "
    I cried in my anguish :
" O once Loved, O fair Unforgotten —
    That Thing — meant it thee !

" Inurned and at peace, lost but sainted,
    Were grief I could compass ;
Depraved — 'tis for Christ's poor dependent
    A cruel decree ! "

I backed on the Highway ; but passed not
    The hostel. Within there
Too mocking to Love's re-expression
    Was Time's repartee !

Uptracking where Legions had wayfared
    By cromlechs unstoried,
And lynchets, and sepultured Chieftains,
    In self-colloquy,

A feeling stirred in me and strengthened
    That *she* was not my Love,
But she of the garth, who lay rapt in
    Her long reverie.

·And thence till to-day I persuade me
   That this was the true one ;
That Death stole intact her young dearness
   And innocency.

Frail-witted, illuded they call me ;
   I may be. Far better
To dream than to own the debasement
   Of sweet Cicely.

Moreover I rate it unseemly
   To hold that kind Heaven
Could work such device — to her ruin
   And my misery.

So, lest I disturb my choice vision,
   I shun the West Highway,
Even now, when the knaps ring with rhythms
   From blackbird and bee ;

And feel that with slumber half-conscious
   She rests in the church-hay,
Her spirit unsoiled as in youth-time
   When lovers were we.

I

I PITCHED my day's leazings in Crimmercrock Lane,
To tie up my garter and jog on again,
When a dear dark-eyed gentleman passed there and
    said,
In a way that made all o' me colour rose-red,
        " What do I see —
        O pretty knee ! "
And he came and he tied up my garter for me.

II

'Twixt sunset and moonrise it was, I can mind :
Ah, 'tis easy to lose what we nevermore find ! —
Of the dear stranger's home, of his name, I knew
    nought,
But I soon knew his nature and all that it brought.
        Then bitterly
        Sobbed I that he
Should ever have tied up my garter for me !

III

Yet now I've beside me a fine lissom lad,
And my slip's nigh forgot, and my days are not sad ;
My own dearest joy is he, comrade, and friend,
He it is who safe-guards me, on him I depend ;
        No sorrow brings he,
        And thankful I be
That his daddy once tied up my garter for me !

NOTE.—"Leazings" (line 1), bundle of gleaned corn.

ONE RALPH BLOSSOM SOLILOQUIZES

("It being deposed that vij women who were mayds before
he knew them have been brought upon the towne [rates ?] by
the fornicacions of one Ralph Blossom, Mr. Maior inquired
why he should not contribute xiv pence weekly toward their
mayntenance. But it being shewn that the sayd R. B. was
dying of a purple feaver, no order was made."—*Budmouth
Borough Minutes:* 16—.)

WHEN I am in hell or some such place,
A-groaning over my sorry case,
What will those seven women say to me
Who, when I coaxed them, answered " Aye " to me ?

" I did not understand your sign ! "
Will be the words of Caroline ;
While Jane will cry, " If I'd had proof of you,
I should have learnt to hold aloof of you ! "

" I won't reproach : it was to be ! "
Will dryly murmur Cicely ;
And Rosa : " I feel no hostility,
For I must own I lent facility."

Lizzy says : " Sharp was my regret,
And sometimes it is now ! But yet
I joy that, though it brought notoriousness,
I knew Love once and all its gloriousness ! "

Says Patience : " Why are we apart ?
Small harm did you, my poor Swect Heart !
A manchild born, now tall and beautiful,
Was worth the ache of days undutiful."

And Anne cries : " O the time was fair,
So wherefore should you burn down there ?
There is a deed under the sun, my Love,
And that was ours. What's done is done, my Love.
These trumpets here in Heaven are dumb to me
With you away. Dear, come, O come to me ! "

ONE WE KNEW

(M. H. 1772–1857)

She told how they used to form for the country
  dances —
    " The Triumph," " The New-rigged Ship "—
To the light of the guttering wax in the panelled
    manses,
      And in cots to the blink of a dip.

She spoke of the wild " poussetting " and " alle-
    manding "
      On carpet, on oak, and on sod ;
And the two long rows of ladies and gentlemen
      standing,
        And the figures the couples trod.

She showed us the spot where the maypole was
      yearly planted,
        And where the bandsmen stood
While breeched and kerchiefed partners whirled,
      and panted
        To choose each other for good.

She told of that far-back day when they learnt
      astounded
        Of the death of the King of France :
Of the Terror ; and then of Bonaparte's unbounded
      Ambition and arrogance.

Of how his threats woke warlike preparations
      Along the southern strand,

And how each night brought tremors and
      trepidations
    Lest morning should see him land.

She said she had often heard the gibbet creaking
    As it swayed in the lightning flash,
Had caught from the neighbouring town a small
      child's shrieking
    At the cart-tail under the lash. . . .

With cap-framed face and long gaze into the
      embers —
    We seated around her knees —
She would dwell on such dead themes, not as one
      who remembers,
    But rather as one who sees.

She seemed one left behind of a band gone distant
    So far that no tongue could hail :
Past things retold were to her as things existent,
    Things present but as a tale.

GEOGRAPHICAL KNOWLEDGE

(A Memory of Christiana C——)

WHERE Blackmoor was, the road that led
    To Bath, she could not show,
Nor point the sky that overspread
    Towns ten miles off or so.

But that Calcutta stood this way,
    Cape Horn there figured fell,
That here was Boston, here Bombay,
    She could declare full well.

Less known to her the track athwart
    Froom Mead or Yell'ham Wood
Than how to make some Austral port
    In seas of surly mood.

She saw the glint of Guinea's shore
    Behind the plum-tree nigh,
Heard old unruly Biscay's roar
    In the weir's purl hard by. . . .

" My son's a sailor, and he knows
    All seas and many lands,
And when he's home he points and shows
    Each country where it stands.

" He's now just there — by Gib's high rock —
    And when he gets, you see,
To Portsmouth here, behind the clock,
    Then he'll come back to me ! "

" WHAT do you see in that time-touched stone,
          When nothing is there
But ashen blankness, although you give it
          A rigid stare ?

" You look not quite as if you saw,
          But as if you heard,
Parting your lips, and treading softly
          As mouse or bird.

" It is only the base of a pillar, they'll tell you
          That came to us
From a far old hill men used to name
          Areopagus."

— " I know no art, and I only view
          A stone from a wall,
But I am thinking that stone has echoed
          The voice of Paul ;

" Paul as he stood and preached beside it
          Facing the crowd,
A small gaunt figure with wasted features,
          Calling out loud

" Words that in all their intimate accents
          Pattered upon
That marble front, and were wide reflected,
          And then were gone.

42

" I'm a labouring man, and know but little,
          Or nothing at all ;
But I can't help thinking that stone once echoed
          The voice of Paul."

THE CONVERGENCE OF THE TWAIN

(Lines on the Loss of the " Titanic ")

I

In a solitude of the sea
Deep from human vanity,
And the Pride of Life that planned her, stilly
couches she.

II

Steel chambers, late the pyres
Of her salamandrine fires,
Cold currents thrid, and turn to rhythmic tidal lyres.

III

Over the mirrors meant
To glass the opulent
The sea-worm crawls — grotesque, slimed, dumb,
indifferent.

IV

Jewels in joy designed
To ravish the sensuous mind
Lie lightless, all their sparkles bleared and black and
blind.

V

Dim moon-eyed fishes near
Gaze at the gilded gear
And query : " What does this vaingloriousness
down here ? " . . .

VI

Well : while was fashioning
This creature of cleaving wing,
The Immanent Will that stirs and urges everything

VII

Prepared a sinister mate
For her — so gaily great —
A Shape of Ice, for the time far and dissociate.

VIII

And as the smart ship grew
In stature, grace, and hue,
In shadowy silent distance grew the Iceberg too.

IX

Alien they seemed to be :
No mortal eye could see
The intimate welding of their later history,

X

Or sign that they were bent
By paths coincident
On being anon twin halves of one august event,

XI

Till the Spinner of the Years
Said " Now ! " And each one hears,
And consummation comes, and jars two hemi-
    spheres.

SHELLEY'S SKYLARK

(The neighbourhood of Leghorn : March 1887)

SOMEWHERE afield here something lies
In Earth's oblivious eyeless trust
That moved a poet to prophecies —
A pinch of unseen, unguarded dust :

The dust of the lark that Shelley heard,
And made immortal through times to be ; —
Though it only lived like another bird,
And knew not its immortality :

Lived its meek life ; then, one day, fell —
A little ball of feather and bone ;
And how it perished, when piped farewell,
And where it wastes, are alike unknown.

Maybe it rests in the loam I view,
Maybe it throbs in a myrtle's green,
Maybe it sleeps in the coming hue
Of a grape on the slopes of yon inland scene.

Go find it, faeries, go and find
That tiny pinch of priceless dust,
And bring a casket silver-lined,
And framed of gold that gems encrust ;

And we will lay it safe therein,
And consecrate it to endless time ;
For it inspired a bard to win
Ecstatic heights in thought and rhyme.

THE SPRING CALL

Down Wessex way, when spring's a-shine,
  The blackbird's " pret-ty de-urr ! "
In Wessex accents marked as mine
  Is heard afar and near.

He flutes it strong, as if in song
  No R's of feebler tone
Than his appear in " pretty dear,"
  Have blackbirds ever known.

Yet they pipe " prattie deerh ! " I glean,
  Beneath a Scottish sky,
And " pehty de-aw ! " amid the treen
  Of Middlesex or nigh.

While some folk say — perhaps in play —
  Who know the Irish isle,
'Tis " purrity dare ! " in treeland there
  When songsters would beguile.

Well : I'll say what the listening birds
  Say, hearing " pret-ty de-urr ! " —
However strangers sound such words,
  That's how we sound them here.

Yes, in this clime at pairing time,
  As soon as eyes can see her
At dawn of day, the proper way
  To call is " pret-ty de-urr ! "

THE LAST SIGNAL

(Oct. 11, 1886)

A Memory of William Barnes

SILENTLY I footed by an uphill road
   That led from my abode to a spot yew-boughed;
Yellowly the sun sloped low down to westward,
         And dark was the east with cloud.

Then, amid the shadow of that livid sad east,
   Where the light was least, and a gate stood wide,
Something flashed the fire of the sun that was
      facing it,
         Like a brief blaze on that side.

Looking hard and harder I knew what it meant —
   The sudden shine sent from the livid east scene;
It meant the west mirrored by the coffin of my
      friend there,
         Turning to the road from his green,

To take his last journey forth — he who in his
      prime
Trudged so many a time from that gate athwart
      the land!
Thus a farewell to me he signalled on his grave-way,
         As with a wave of his hand.

WINTERBORNE-CAME PATH

48

OVERLOOKING THE RIVER STOUR

THE swallows flew in the curves of an eight
      Above the river-gleam
      In the wet June's last beam :
Like little crossbows animate
The swallows flew in the curves of an eight
      Above the river-gleam.

Planing up shavings of crystal spray
      A moor-hen darted out
      From the bank thereabout,
And through the stream-shine ripped her way ;
Planing up shavings of crystal spray
      A moor-hen darted out.

Closed were the kingcups ; and the mead
      Dripped in monotonous green,
      Though the day's morning sheen
Had shown it golden and honeybee'd ;
Closed were the kingcups ; and the mead
      Dripped in monotonous green.

And never I turned my head, alack,
      While these things met my gaze
      Through the pane's drop-drenched glaze,
To see the more behind my back. . . .
O never I turned, but let, alack,
      These less things hold my gaze !

ON STURMINSTER FOOT-BRIDGE

(Onomatopœic)

RETICULATIONS creep upon the slack stream's face
  When the wind skims irritably past,
The current clucks smartly into each hollow place
That years of flood have scrabbled in the pier's
        sodden base ;
    The floating-lily leaves rot fast.

On a roof stand the swallows ranged in wistful
        waiting rows,
    Till they arrow off and drop like stones
Among the eyot-withies at whose foot the river
        flows :
And beneath the roof is she who in the dark world
        shows
    As a lattice-gleam when midnight moans.

THE MAN WHO FORGOT

At a lonely cross where bye-roads met
   I sat upon a gate ;
I saw the sun decline and set,
   And still was fain to wait.

A trotting boy passed up the way
   And roused me from my thought ;
I called to him, and showed where lay
   A spot I shyly sought.

" A summer-house fair stands hidden where
   You see the moonlight thrown ;
Go, tell me if within it there
   A lady sits alone."

He half demurred, but took the track,
   And silence held the scene ;
I saw his figure rambling back ;
   I asked him if he had been.

" I went just where you said, but found
   No summer-house was there :
Beyond the slope 'tis all bare ground ;
   Nothing stands anywhere.

" A man asked what my brains were worth ;
   The house, he said, grew rotten,
And was pulled down before my birth,
   And is almost forgotten ! "

My right mind woke, and I stood dumb ;
   Forty years' frost and flower
Had fleeted since I'd used to come
   To meet her in that bower.

A NIGHT IN NOVEMBER

I MARKED when the weather changed,
And the panes began to quake,
And the winds rose up and ranged,
That night, lying half-awake.

Dead leaves blew into my room,
And alighted upon my bed,
And a tree declared to the gloom
Its sorrow that they were shed.

One leaf of them touched my hand,
And I thought that it was you
There stood as you used to stand,
And saying at last you knew!

ROYAL SPONSORS

" THE king and the queen will stand to the child ;
    'Twill be handed down in song ;
And it's no more than their deserving,
With my lord so faithful at Court so long,
        And so staunch and strong.

" O never before was known such a thing !
    'Twill be a grand time for all ;
And the beef will be a whole-roast bullock,
And the servants will have a feast in the hall,
        And the ladies a ball.

" While from Jordan's stream by a traveller,
    In a flagon of silver wrought,
And by caravan, stage-coach, wain, and waggon
A precious trickle has been brought,
        Clear as when caught."

The morning came.   To the park of the peer
    The royal couple bore ;
And the font was filled with the Jordan water,
And the household awaited their guests before
        The carpeted door.

But when they went to the silk-lined cot
    The child was found to have died.
" What's now to be done ?   We can disappoint not
The king and queen ! " the family cried
        With eyes spread wide.

" Even now they approach the chestnut-drive !
    The service must be read."
" Well, since we can't christen the child alive,
By God we shall have to christen him dead ! "
    The marquis said.

Thus, breath-forsaken, a corpse was taken
    To the private chapel — yea —
And the king knew not, nor the queen, God wot,
That they answered for one returned to clay
    At the font that day.

THE CHAPEL-ORGANIST

(A.D. 185–)

I'VE been thinking it through, as I play here to-
    night, to play never again,
By the light of that lowering sun peering in at the
    window-pane,
And over the back-street roofs, throwing shades
    from the boys of the chore
In the gallery, right upon me, sitting up to those
    keys once more. . . .

How I used to hear tongues ask, as I sat here when
    I was new :
" Who is she playing the organ ? She touches it
    mightily true ! "
" She travels from Havenpool Town," the deacon
    would softly speak,
" The stipend can hardly cover her fare hither twice
    in the week."
(It fell far short of doing, indeed ; but I never told,
For I have craved minstrelsy more than lovers, or
    beauty, or gold.)

'Twas so he answered at first, but the story grew
    different later :
" It cannot go on much longer, from what we hear
    of her now ! "
At the meaning wheeze in the words the inquirer
    would shift his place
Till he could see round the curtain that screened me
    from people below.
" A handsome girl," he would murmur, upstaring,
    (and so I am).

" But — too much sex in her build ; fine eyes, but
    eyelids too heavy ;
A bosom too full for her age ; in her lips too
    voluptuous a dye."
(It may be. But who put it there ? Assuredly it
    was not I.)

I went on playing and singing when this I had
    heard, and more,
Though tears half-blinded me ; yes, I remained
    going on and on,
Just as I used me to chord and to sing at the self-
    same time ! . . .
For it's a contralto — my voice is ; they'll hear it
    again here to-night
In the psalmody notes that I love far beyond every
    lower delight.

Well, the deacon, in fact, that day had learnt new
    tidings about me ;
They troubled his mind not a little, for he was a
    worthy man.
(He trades as a chemist in High Street, and during
    the week he had sought
His fellow-deacon, who throve as a bookbinder
    over the way.)
" These are strange rumours," he said. " We must
    guard the good name of the chapel.
If, sooth, she's of evil report, what else can we do
    but dismiss her ? "
" — But get such another to play here we cannot
    for double the price ! "
It settled the point for the time, and I triumphed
    awhile in their strait,

And my much-beloved grand semibreves went
    living on, pending my fate.

At length in the congregation more headshakes and
    murmurs were rife,
And my dismissal was ruled, though I was not
    warned of it then.
But a day came when they declared it. The news
    entered me as a sword ;
I was broken ; so pallid of face that they thought I
    should faint, they said.
I rallied. " O, rather than go, I will play you for
    nothing ! " said I.
'Twas in much desperation I spoke it, for bring me
    to forfeit I could not
Those melodies chorded so richly for which I had
    laboured and lived.
They paused. And for nothing I played at the
    chapel through Sundays again,
Upheld by that art which I loved more than bland-
    ishments lavished of men.

But it fell that murmurs anew from the flock broke
    the pastor's peace.
Some member had seen me at Havenpool, comrading
    close a sea-captain.
(O yes ; I was thereto constrained, lacking means
    for the fare to and fro.)
Yet God knows, if aught He knows ever, I loved
    the Old-Hundredth, Saint Stephen's,
Mount Zion, New Sabbath, Miles-Lane, Holy Rest,
    and Arabia, and Eaton,
Above all embraces of body by wooers who sought
    me and won ! . . .

Next week 'twas declared I was seen coming home
    with a swain ere the sun.
The deacons insisted then, strong ; and forgiveness
    I did not implore.
I saw all was lost for me, quite, but I made a last
    bid in my throbs.
My bent, finding victual in lust, men's senses had
    libelled my soul,
But the soul should die game, if I knew it ! I
    turned to my masters and said :
" I yield, Gentlemen, without parlance. But — let
    me just hymn you *once* more !
It's a little thing, Sirs, that I ask ; and a passion is
    music with me ! "
They saw that consent would cost nothing, and
    show as good grace, as knew I,
Though tremble I did, and feel sick, as I paused
    thereat, dumb for their words.
They gloomily nodded assent, saying, " Yes, if you
    care to. Once more,
And only once more, understand." To that with a
    bend I agreed.
— " You've a fixed and a far-reaching look," spoke
    one who had eyed me awhile.
" I've a fixed and a far-reaching plan, and my look
    only showed it," I smile.

This evening of Sunday is come — the last of my
    functioning here.
" She plays as if she were possessed ! " they exclaim
    glancing upward and round.
" Such harmonies I never dreamt the old instrumen
    capable of ! "

Meantime the sun lowers and goes ; shades deepen ;
    the lights are turned up,
And the people voice out the last singing : tune
    Tallis : the Evening Hymn.
(I wonder Dissenters sing Ken : it shows them
    more liberal in spirit
At this little chapel down here than at certain new
    others I know.)
I sing as I play. Murmurs some one : " No woman's
    throat richer than hers ! "
" True : in these parts," think I. " But, my man,
    never more will its richness outspread."
And I sing with them onward : " The grave dread
    as little do I as my bed."

I lift up my feet from the pedals ; and then, while
    my eyes are still wet
From the symphonies born of my fingers, I do that
    whereon I am set,
And draw from my " full round bosom," (their
    words ; how can I help its heave ?)
A bottle blue-coloured and fluted — a vinaigrette,
    they may conceive —
And before the choir measures my meaning, reads
    aught in my moves to and fro,
I drink from the phial at a draught, and they think
    it a pick-me-up ; so.

Then I gather my books as to leave, bend over the
    keys as to pray.
When they come to me motionless, stooping, quick
    death will have whisked me away.

" Sure, nobody meant her to poison herself in her
    haste, after all ! "
The deacons will say as they carry me down and
    the night-shadows fall,
" Though the charges were true," they will add.
    " It's a case red as scarlet withal ! "
I have never once minced it.   Lived chaste I have
    not.   Heaven knows it above ! . . .
But past all the heavings of passion — it's music has
    been my life-love ! . . .
That tune did go well — this last playing ! . . . I
    reckon they'll bury me here. . . .
Not a soul from the seaport my birthplace — will
    come, or bestow me . . . a tear.

THE CONTRETEMPS

A FORWARD rush by the lamp in the gloom,
　　And we clasped, and almost kissed;
But she was not the woman whom
I had promised to meet in the thawing brume
On that harbour-bridge; nor was I he of her
　　　　tryst.

So loosening from me swift she said:
　　" O why, why feign to be
The one I had meant! — to whom I have sped
To fly with, being so sorrily wed! "
— 'Twas thus and thus that she upbraided me.

My assignation had struck upon
　　Some others' like it, I found.
And her lover rose on the night anon;
And then her husband entered on
The lamplit, snowflaked, sloppiness around.

" Take her and welcome, man! " he cried:
　　" I wash my hands of her.
I'll find me twice as good a bride! "
— All this to me, whom he had eyed,
Plainly, as his wife's planned deliverer.

And next the lover: " Little I knew,
　　Madam, you had a third!
Kissing here in my very view! "
— Husband and lover then withdrew.
I let them; and I told them not they erred.

Why not ?   Well, there faced she and I —
    Two strangers who'd kissed, or near,
Chancewise.   To see stand weeping by
A woman once embraced, will try
The tension of a man the most austere.

So it began ; and I was young,
    She pretty, by the lamp,
As flakes came waltzing down among
The waves of her clinging hair, that hung
Heavily on her temples, dark and damp.

And there alone still stood we two ;
    She one cast off for me,
Or so it seemed : while night ondrew,
Forcing a parley what should do
We twain hearts caught in one catastrophe.

In stranded souls a common strait
    Wakes latencies unknown,
Whose impulse may precipitate
A life-long leap.   The hour was late,
And there was the Jersey boat with its funnel
        agroan.

" Is wary walking worth much pother ? "
    It grunted, as still it stayed.
" One pairing is as good as another
Where all is venture !   Take each other,
And scrap the oaths that you have aforetime
        made." . . .

— Of the four involved there walks but one
   On earth at this late day.
And what of the chapter so begun?
In that odd complex what was done?
Well; happiness comes in full to none:
Let peace lie on lulled lips: I will not say.

WEYMOUTH

WE shall see her no more
        On the balcony,
Smiling, while hurt, at the roar
        As of surging sea
From the stormy sturdy band
        Who have doomed her lord's cause,
Though she waves her little hand
        As it were applause.

Here will be candidates yet,
        And candidates' wives,
Fervid with zeal to set
        Their ideals on our lives :
Here will come market-men
        On the market-days,
Here will clash now and then
        More such party assays.

And the balcony will fill
        When such times are renewed,
And the throng in the street will thrill
        With to-day's mettled mood ;
But she will no more stand
        In the sunshine there,
With that wave of her white-gloved hand,
        And that chestnut hair.

January 1906

"MEN WHO MARCH AWAY"

(Song of the Soldiers)

WHAT of the faith and fire within us
      Men who march away
      Ere the barn-cocks say
      Night is growing gray,
Leaving all that here can win us ;
What of the faith and fire within us
      Men who march away ?

Is it a purblind prank, O think you,
      Friend with the musing eye,
      Who watch us stepping by
      With doubt and dolorous sigh ?
Can much pondering so hoodwink you !
Is it a purblind prank, O think you,
      Friend with the musing eye ?

Nay. We well see what we are doing,
      Though some may not see —
      Dalliers as they be —
      England's need are we ;
Her distress would leave us rueing :
Nay. We well see what we are doing,
      Though some may not see !

In our heart of hearts believing
      Victory crowns the just,
      And that braggarts must
      Surely bite the dust,
Press we to the field ungrieving,
In our heart of hearts believing
      Victory crowns the just.

Hence the faith and fire within us
    Men who march away
    Ere the barn-cocks say
    Night is growing gray,
Leaving all that here can win us ;
Hence the faith and fire within us
    Men who march away.

September 5, 1914

I

ONLY a man harrowing clods
In a slow silent walk
With an old horse that stumbles and nods
Half asleep as they stalk.

II

Only thin smoke without flame
From the heaps of couch-grass ;
Yet this will go onward the same
Though Dynasties pass.

III

Yonder a maid and her wight
Come whispering by :
War's annals will cloud into night
Ere their story die.

1915

[1] Jer. li. 20.

JEZREEL

On its Seizure by the English under Allenby,
September 1918

Did they catch as it were in a Vision at shut of the
    day —
When their cavalry smote through the ancient
    Esdraelon Plain,
And they crossed where the Tishbite stood forth in
    his enemy's way —
His gaunt mournful Shade as he bade the King
    haste off amain ?

On war-men at this end of time — even on English-
    men's eyes —
Who slay with their arms of new might in that
    long-ago place,
Flashed he who drove furiously ? . . . Ah, did the
    phantom arise
Of that queen, of that proud Tyrian woman who
    painted her face ?

Faintly marked they the words " Throw her
    down ! " from the Night eerily,
Spectre-spots of the blood of her body on some
    rotten wall ?
And the thin note of pity that came : " A King's
    daughter is she,"
As they passed where she trodden was once by the
    chargers' footfall ?

Could such be the hauntings of men of to-day, at
    the cease

Of pursuit, at the dusk-hour, ere slumber their
    senses could seal ?
Enghosted seers, kings — one on horseback who
    asked " Is it peace ? " . . .
Yea, strange things and spectral may men have
    beheld in Jezreel !

POEMS OF MEMORY AND
REFLECTION

" WHEN I SET OUT FOR LYONNESSE "

(1870)

When I set out for Lyonnesse,
    A hundred miles away,
    The rime was on the spray,
And starlight lit my lonesomeness
When I set out for Lyonnesse
    A hundred miles away.

What would bechance at Lyonnesse
    While I should sojourn there
    No prophet durst declare,
Nor did the wisest wizard guess
What would bechance at Lyonnesse
    While I should sojourn there.

When I came back from Lyonnesse
    With magic in my eyes,
    All marked with mute surmise
My radiance rare and fathomless,
When I came back from Lyonnesse
    With magic in my eyes !

I TRAVEL on by barren farms,
And gulls glint out like silver flecks
Against a cloud that speaks of wrecks,
And bellies down with black alarms.
I say : " Thus from my lady's arms
I go ; those arms I love the best ! "
The wind replies from dip and rise,
" Nay ; toward her arms thou journeyest."

A distant verge morosely gray
Appears, while clots of flying foam
Break from its muddy monochrome,
And a light blinks up far away.
I sigh : " My eyes now as all day
Behold her ebon loops of hair ! "
Like bursting bonds the wind responds,
" Nay, wait for tresses flashing fair ! "

From tides the lofty coastlands screen
Come smitings like the slam of doors,
Or hammerings on hollow floors,
As the swell cleaves through caves unseen.
Say I : " Though broad this wild terrene,
Her city home is matched of none ! "
From the hoarse skies the wind replies :
" Thou shouldst have said her sea-board one."

The all-prevailing clouds exclude
The one quick timorous transient star ;
The waves outside where breakers are
Huzza like a mad multitude.

" Where the sun ups it, mist-imbued,"
I cry, " there reigns the star for me ! "
The wind outshrieks from points and peaks :
" Here, westward, where it downs, mean ye ! "

Yonder the headland, vulturine,
Snores like old Skrymer in his sleep,
And every chasm and every steep
Blackens as wakes each pharos-shine.
" I roam, but one is safely mine,"
I say.   " God grant she stay my own ! "
Low laughs the wind as if it grinned :
" Thy Love is one thou'st not yet known."

THE TEMPORARY THE ALL
(Sapphics)

CHANGE and chancefulness in my flowering youth-
time,
Set me sun by sun near to one unchosen;
Wrought us fellowlike, and despite divergence,
　　　　Fused us in friendship.

" Cherish him can I while the true one forthcome —
Come the rich fulfiller of my prevision;
Life is roomy yet, and the odds unbounded."
　　　　So self-communed I.

'Thwart my wistful way did a damsel saunter,
Fair, albeit unformed to be all-eclipsing;
" Maiden meet," held I, " till arise my forefelt
　　　　Wonder of women."

Long a visioned hermitage deep desiring,
Tenements uncouth I was fain to house in:
" Let such lodging be for a breath-while," thought I,
　　　　" Soon a more seemly.

" Then high handiwork will I make my life-deed,
Truth and Light outshow; but the ripe time pending,
Intermissive aim at the thing sufficeth."
　　　　Thus I. . . . But lo, me!

Mistress, friend, place, aims to be bettered straight-
way,
Bettered not has Fate or my hand's achievement;
Sole the showance those of my onward earth-track —
　　　　Never transcended!

A YOUNG MAN'S EXHORTATION

CALL off your eyes from care
By some determined deftness ; put forth joys
Dear as excess without the core that cloys,
 And charm Life's lourings fair.

Exalt and crown the hour
That girdles us, and fill it full with glee,
Blind glee, excelling aught could ever be
 Were heedfulness in power.

Send up such touching strains
That limitless recruits from Fancy's pack
Shall rush upon your tongue, and tender back
 All that your soul contains.

For what do we know best ?
That a fresh love-leaf crumpled soon will dry,
And that men moment after moment die,
 Of all scope dispossest.

If I have seen one thing
It is the passing preciousness of dreams ;
That aspects are within us ; and who seems
 Most kingly is the King.

1867 : WESTBOURNE PARK VILLAS

THE COMET AT YELL'HAM

I

It bends far over Yell'ham Plain,
  And we, from Yell'ham Height,
Stand and regard its fiery train,
  So soon to swim from sight.

II

It will return long years hence, when
  As now its strange swift shine
Will fall on Yell'ham; but not then
  On that sweet form of thine.

IN A CATHEDRAL CITY

THESE people have not heard your name;
No loungers in this placid place
Have helped to bruit your beauty's fame.

The grey Cathedral, towards whose face
Bend eyes untold, has met not yours;
Your shade has never swept its base,

Your form has never darked its doors,
Nor have your faultless feet once thrown
A pensive pit-pat on its floors.

Along the street to maids well known
Blithe lovers hum their tender airs,
But in your praise voice not a tone. . . .

— Since nought bespeaks you here, or bears,
As I, your imprint through and through,
Here might I rest, till my heart shares
The spot's unconsciousness of you!

SALISBURY

THE YEAR'S AWAKENING

How do you know that the pilgrim track
Along the belting zodiac
Swept by the sun in his seeming rounds
Is traced by now to the Fishes' bounds
And into the Ram, when weeks of cloud
Have wrapt the sky in a clammy shroud,
And never as yet a tinct of spring
Has shown in the Earth's apparelling ;
    O vespering bird, how do you know,
      How do you know ?

How do you know, deep underground,
Hid in your bed from sight and sound,
Without a turn in temperature,
With weather life can scarce endure,
That light has won a fraction's strength,
And day put on some moments' length,
Whereof in merest rote will come,
Weeks hence, mild airs that do not numb ;
    O crocus root, how do you know,
      How do you know ?

UNDER THE WATERFALL

" WHENEVER I plunge my arm, like this,
In a basin of water, I never miss
The sweet sharp sense of a fugitive day
Fetched back from its thickening shroud of gray.
      Hence the only prime
      And real love-rhyme
      That I know by heart,
      And that leaves no smart,
Is the purl of a little valley fall
About three spans wide and two spans tall
Over a table of solid rock,
And into a scoop of the self-same block ;
The purl of a runlet that never ceases
In stir of kingdoms, in wars, in peaces ;
With a hollow boiling voice it speaks
And has spoken since hills were turfless peaks."

" And why gives this the only prime
Idea to you of a real love-rhyme ?
And why does plunging your arm in a bowl
Full of spring water, bring throbs to your soul ? "

" Well, under the fall, in a crease of the stone,
Though where precisely none ever has known,
Jammed darkly, nothing to show how prized,
And by now with its smoothness opalized,
      Is a drinking-glass :
      For, down that pass
      My lover and I
      Walked under a sky
Of blue with a leaf-wove awning of green,

In the burn of August, to paint the scene,
And we placed our basket of fruit and wine
By the runlet's rim, where we sat to dine ;
And when we had drunk from the glass together,
Arched by the oak-copse from the weather,
I held the vessel to rinse in the fall,
Where it slipped, and sank, and was past recall,
Though we stooped and plumbed the little abyss
With long bared arms.   There the glass still is.
And, as said, if I thrust my arm below
Cold water in basin or bowl, a throe
From the past awakens a sense of that time,
And the glass we used, and the cascade's rhyme.
The basin seems the pool, and its edge
The hard smooth face of the brook-side ledge,
And the leafy pattern of china-ware
The hanging plants that were bathing there.

" By night, by day, when it shines or lours,
There lies intact that chalice of ours,
And its presence adds to the rhyme of love
Persistently sung by the fall above.
No lip has touched it since his and mine
In turns therefrom sipped lovers' wine."

GREAT THINGS

Sweet cyder is a great thing,
   A great thing to me,
Spinning down to Weymouth town
   By Ridgway thirstily,
And maid and mistress summoning
   Who tend the hostelry :
O cyder is a great thing,
   A great thing to me !

The dance it is a great thing,
   A great thing to me,
With candles lit and partners fit
   For night-long revelry ;
And going home when day-dawning
   Peeps pale upon the lea :
O dancing is a great thing,
   A great thing to me !

Love is, yea, a great thing,
   A great thing to me,
When, having drawn across the lawn
   In darkness silently,
A figure flits like one a-wing
   Out from the nearest tree :
O love is, yes, a great thing,
   A great thing to me !

Will these be always great things,
   Great things to me ? . . .
Let it befall that One will call,
   " Soul, I have need of thee : "

What then? Joy-jaunts, impassioned flings,
    Love, and its ecstasy,
Will always have been great things,
    Great things to me!

A THOUGHT IN TWO MOODS

I saw it — pink and white — revealed
   Upon the white and green ;
The white and green was a daisied field,
   The pink and white Ethleen.

And as I looked it seemed in kind
   That difference they had none ;
The two fair bodiments combined
   As varied miens of one.

A sense that, in some mouldering year,
   As one they both would lie,
Made me move quickly on to her
   To pass the pale thought by.

She laughed and said : " Out there, to me,
   You looked so weather-browned,
And brown in clothes, you seemed to be
   Made of the dusty ground ! "

THE CHIMES

THAT morning when I trod the town
The twitching chimes of long renown
    Played out to me
The sweet Sicilian sailors' tune,
And I knew not if late or soon
    My day would be :

A day of sunshine beryl-bright
And windless ; yea, think as I might,
    I could not say,
Even to within years' measure, when
One would be at my side who then
    Was far away.

When hard utilitarian times
Had stilled the sweet Saint-Peter's chimes
    I learnt to see
That bale may spring where blisses are,
And one desired might be afar
    Though near to me.

WEATHERS

I

This is the weather the cuckoo likes,
     And so do I;
When showers betumble the chestnut spikes,
     And nestlings fly:
And the little brown nightingale bills his best,
And they sit outside at " The Travellers' Rest,"
And maids come forth sprig-muslin drest,
And citizens dream of the south and west,
     And so do I.

II

This is the weather the shepherd shuns,
     And so do I;
When beeches drip in browns and duns,
     And thresh, and ply;
And hill-hid tides throb, throe on throe,
And meadow rivulets overflow,
And drops on gate-bars hang in a row,
And rooks in families homeward go,
     And so do I.

THE BULLFINCHES

BROTHER Bulleys, let us sing
From the dawn till evening ! —
For we know not that we go not
    When to-day's pale pinions fold
    Where they be that sang of old.

When I flew to Blackmoor Vale,
Whence the green-gowned faeries hail,
Roosting near them I could hear them
    Speak of queenly Nature's ways,
    Means, and moods, — well known to fays.

All we creatures, nigh and far
(Said they there), the Mother's are ;
Yet she never shows endeavour
    To protect from warrings wild
    Bird or beast she calls her child.

Busy in her handsome house
Known as Space, she falls a-drowse ;
Yet, in seeming, works on dreaming,
    While beneath her groping hands
    Fiends make havoc in her bands.

How her hussif'ry succeeds
She unknows or she unheeds,
All things making for Death's taking !
    — So the green-gowned faeries say
    Living over Blackmoor way.

Come then, brethren, let us sing,
    From the dawn till evening ! —
For we know not that we go not
    When the day's pale pinions fold
    Where those be that sang of old.

THE DARKLING THRUSH

I LEANT upon a coppice gate
    When Frost was spectre-gray,
And Winter's dregs made desolate
    The weakening eye of day.
The tangled bine-stems scored the sky
    Like strings of broken lyres,
And all mankind that haunted nigh
    Had sought their household fires.

The land's sharp features seemed to be
    The Century's corpse outleant,
His crypt the cloudy canopy,
    The wind his death-lament.
The ancient pulse of germ and birth
    Was shrunken hard and dry,
And every spirit upon earth
    Seemed fervourless as I.

At once a voice arose among
    The bleak twigs overhead
In a full-hearted evensong
    Of joy illimited ;
An aged thrush, frail, gaunt, and small,
    In blast-beruffled plume,
Had chosen thus to fling his soul
    Upon the growing gloom.

So little cause for carollings
    Of such ecstatic sound
Was written on terrestrial things
    Afar or nigh around,

That I could think there trembled through
    His happy good-night air
Some blessed Hope, whereof he knew
    And I was unaware.

  31st December 1900

"More than one cuckoo?"
And the little boy
Seemed to lose something
Of his spring joy.

When he'd grown up
He told his son
He'd used to think
There was only one,

Who came each year
With the trees' new trim
On purpose to please
England and him:

And his son — old already
In life and its ways —
Said yawning: "How foolish
Boys were in those days!"

SUMMER SCHEMES

WHEN friendly summer calls again,
    Calls again
Her little fifers to these hills,
We'll go — we two — to that arched fane
Of leafage where they prime their bills
Before they start to flood the plain
With quavers, minims, shakes, and trills.
    " — We'll go," I sing ; but who shall say
    What may not chance before that day !

And we shall see the waters spring,
    Waters spring
From chinks the scrubby copses crown ;
And we shall trace their oncreeping
To where the cascade tumbles down
And sends the bobbing growths aswing,
And ferns not quite but almost drown.
    " — We shall," I say ; but who may sing
    Of what another moon will bring !

BEFORE AND AFTER SUMMER

I

LOOKING forward to the spring
One puts up with anything.
On this February day
Though the winds leap down the street
Wintry scourgings seem but play,
And these later shafts of sleet,
— Sharper pointed than the first —
And these later snows — the worst —
Are as a half-transparent blind
Riddled by rays from sun behind.

II

Shadows of the October pine
Reach into this room of mine :
On the pine there swings a bird ;
He is shadowed with the tree.
Mutely perched he bills no word ;
Blank as I am even is he.
For those happy suns are past,
Fore-discerned in winter last.
When went by their pleasure, then ?
I, alas, perceived not when.

THE SOMETHING THAT SAVED HIM

IT was when
Whirls of thick waters laved me
    Again and again,
That something arose and saved me;
    Yea, it was then.

    In that day
Unseeing the azure went I
    On my way,
And to white winter bent I,
    Knowing no May.

    Reft of renown,
Under the night clouds beating
    Up and down,
In my needfulness greeting
    Cit and clown.

    Long there had been
Much of a murky colour
    In the scene,
Dull prospects meeting duller;
    Nought between.

    Last, there loomed
A closing-in blind alley,
    Though there boomed
A feeble summons to rally
    Where it gloomed.

The clock rang;
The hour brought a hand to deliver;
    I upsprang,
And looked back at den, ditch and river,
    And sang.

WHILE DRAWING IN A CHURCHYARD

" It is sad that so many of worth,
　　Still in the flesh," soughed the yew,
" Misjudge their lot whom kindly earth
　　　　Secludes from view.

" They ride their diurnal round
　　Each day-span's sum of hours
In peerless ease, without jolt or bound
　　　　Or ache like ours.

" If the living could but hear
　　What is heard by my roots as they creep
Round the restful flock, and the things said there
　　　　No one would weep."

" ' Now set among the wise,'
　　They say : ' Enlarged in scope,
That no God trumpet us to rise
　　　　We truly hope.' "

I listened to his strange tale
　　In the mood that stillness brings,
And I grew to accept as the day wore pale
　　　　That show of things.

Upon a poet's page I wrote
Of old two letters of her name;
Part seemed she of the effulgent thought
Whence that high singer's rapture came.
— When now I turn the leaf the same
Immortal light illumes the lay,
But from the letters of her name
The radiance has waned away!

1869

SHE, TO HIM

I

WHEN you shall see me in the toils of Time,
My lauded beauties carried off from me,
My eyes no longer stars as in their prime,
My name forgot of Maiden Fair and Free;

When, in your being, heart concedes to mind,
And judgment, though you scarce its process know,
Recalls the excellencies I once enshrined,
And you are irked that they have withered so:

Remembering mine the loss is, not the blame,
That Sportsman Time but rears his brood to kill,
Knowing me in my soul the very same —
One who would die to spare you touch of ill! —
Will you not grant to old affection's claim
The hand of friendship down Life's sunless hill?

1866

II

PERHAPS, long hence, when I have passed away,
Some other's feature, accent, thought like mine,
Will carry you back to what I used to say,
And bring some memory of your love's decline.

Then you may pause awhile and think, " Poor
    jade ! "
And yield a sigh to me — as ample due,
Not as the tittle of a debt unpaid
To one who could resign her all to you —

And thus reflecting, you will never see
That your thin thought, in two small words
    conveyed,
Was no such fleeting phantom-thought to me,
But the Whole Life wherein my part was played ;
And you amid its fitful masquerade
A Thought — as I in your life seem to be !

1866

SHE, TO HIM

III

I WILL be faithful to thee ; aye, I will !
And Death shall choose me with a wondering eye
That he did not discern and domicile
One his by right ever since that last Good-bye !

I have no care for friends, or kin, or prime
Of manhood who deal gently with me here ;
Amid the happy people of my time
Who work their love's fulfilment, I appear

Numb as a vane that cankers on its point,
True to the wind that kissed ere canker came :
Despised by souls of Now, who would disjoint
The mind from memory, making Life all aim,

My old dexterities in witchery gone,
And nothing left for Love to look upon.

1866

Upon a noon I pilgrimed through
    A pasture, mile by mile,
Unto the place where last I saw
    My dead Love's living smile.

And sorrowing I lay me down
    Upon the heated sod :
It seemed as if my body pressed
    The very ground she trod.

I lay, and thought ; and in a trance
    She came and stood thereby —
The same, even to the marvellous ray
    That used to light her eye.

" You draw me, and I come to you,
    My faithful one," she said,
In voice that had the moving tone
    It bore ere she was wed.

" Seven years have circled since I died :
    Few now remember me ;
My husband clasps another bride :
    My children's love has she.

" My brethren, sisters, and my friends
    Care not to meet my sprite :
Who prized me most I did not know
    Till I passed down from sight."

I said : " My days are lonely here ;
      I need thy smile alway :
I'll use this night my ball or blade,
      And join thee ere the day."

A tremor stirred her tender lips,
      Which parted to dissuade :
" That cannot be, O friend," she cried ;
      " Think, I am but a Shade !

" A Shade but in its mindful ones
      Has immortality ;
By living, me you keep alive,
      By dying you slay me.

" In you resides my single power
      Of sweet continuance here ;
On your fidelity I count
      Through many a coming year."

— I started through me at her plight,
      So suddenly confessed :
Dismissing late distaste for life,
      I craved its bleak unrest.

" I will not die, my One of all ! —
      To lengthen out thy days
I'll guard me from minutest harms
      That may invest my ways ! "

She smiled and went. Since then she comes
      Oft when her birth-moon climbs,
Or at the seasons' ingresses,
      Or anniversary times ;

But grows my grief.   When I surcease,
    Through whom alone lives she,
Her spirit ends its living lease,
    Never again to be !

THE SHADOW ON THE STONE

I WENT by the Druid stone
  That broods in the garden white and lone,
And I stopped and looked at the shifting shadows
  That at some moments fall thereon
  From the tree hard by with a rhythmic swing,
  And they shaped in my imagining
To the shade that a well-known head and shoulders
  Threw there when she was gardening.

  I thought her behind my back,
  Yea, her I long had learned to lack,
And I said: " I am sure you are standing behind
      me,
  Though how do you get into this old track ? "
  And there was no sound but the fall of a leaf
  As a sad response ; and to keep down grief
I would not turn my head to discover
  That there was nothing in my belief.

  Yet I wanted to look and see
  That nobody stood at the back of me ;
But I thought once more : " Nay, I'll not unvision
  A shape which, somehow, there may be."
  So I went on softly from the glade,
  And left her behind me throwing her shade,
As she were indeed an apparition —
  My head unturned lest my dream should fade.

To M. H.

WE passed where flag and flower
Signalled a jocund throng;
We said: " Go to, the hour
Is apt ! " — and joined the song;
And, kindling, laughed at life and care,
Although we knew no laugh lay there.

We walked where shy birds stood
Watching us, wonder-dumb;
Their friendship met our mood;
We cried: " We'll often come:
We'll come morn, noon, eve, everywhen ! "
— We doubted we should come again.

We joyed to see strange sheens
Leap from quaint leaves in shade;
A secret light of greens
They'd for their pleasure made.
We said: " We'll set such sorts as these ! "
— We knew with night the wish would cease.

" So sweet the place," we said,
" Its tacit tales so dear,
Our thoughts, when breath has sped,
Will meet and mingle here ! " . . .
" Words ! " mused we. " Passed the mortal door,
Our thoughts will reach this nook no more."

THE CONFORMERS

Yes; we'll wed, my little fay,
    And you shall write you mine,
And in a villa chastely gray
    We'll house, and sleep, and dine.
    But those night-screened, divine,
    Stolen trysts of heretofore,
We of choice ecstasies and fine
        Shall know no more.

The formal-faced cohue
    Will then no more upbraid
With smiting smiles and whisperings two
    Who have thrown less loves in shade.
    We shall no more evade
    The searching light of the sun,
Our game of passion will be played,
        Our dreaming done.

We shall not go in stealth
    To rendezvous unknown,
But friends will ask me of your health,
    And you about my own.
    When we abide alone,
    No leapings each to each,
But syllables in frigid tone
        Of household speech.

When down to dust we glide
    Men will not say askance,
As now: "How all the country side
    Rings with their mad romance!"

But as they graveward glance
Remark : " In them we lose
A worthy pair, who helped advance
Sound parish views."

FRIENDS BEYOND

WILLIAM DEWY, Tranter Reuben, Farmer Ledlow
　　　late at plough,
　　　　Robert's kin, and John's, and Ned's,
And the Squire, and Lady Susan, lie in Mellstock
　　　churchyard now !

" Gone," I call them, gone for good, that group of
　　　local hearts and heads ;
　　　　Yet at mothy curfew-tide,
And at midnight when the noon-heat breathes it
　　　back from walls and leads,

They've a way of whispering to me — fellow-wight
　　　who yet abide —
　　　　In the muted, measured note
Of a ripple under archways, or a lone cave's
　　　stillicide :

" We have triumphed : this achievement turns the
　　　bane to antidote,
　　　　Unsuccesses to success,
Many thought-worn eves and morrows to a morrow
　　　free of thought.

" No more need we corn and clothing, feel of old
　　　terrestrial stress ;
　　　　Chill detraction stirs no sigh ;
Fear of death has even bygone us : death gave all
　　　that we possess."

W. D.—" Ye mid burn the old bass-viol that I set
      such value by."
Squire.—" You may hold the manse in fee,
      You may wed my spouse, may let my children's
      memory of me die."

Lady S.—" You may have my rich brocades, my
      laces ; take each household key ;
    Ransack coffer, desk, bureau ;
    Quiz the few poor treasures hid there, con the
      letters kept by me."

Far.—" Ye mid zell my favourite heifer, ye mid let
      the charlock grow,
    Foul the grinterns, give up thrift."
Far. Wife.—" If ye break my best blue china,
      children, I shan't care or ho."

All.—" We've no wish to hear the tidings, how the
      people's fortunes shift ;
    What your daily doings are ;
    Who are wedded, born, divided ; if your lives
      beat slow or swift.

" Curious not the least are we if our intents you
      make or mar,
    If you quire to our old tune,
If the City stage still passes, if the weirs still roar
      afar."

— Thus, with very gods' composure, freed those
      crosses late and soon
    Which, in life, the Trine allow
(Why, none witteth), and ignoring all that haps
      beneath the moon,

William Dewy, Tranter Reuben, Farmer Ledlow
      late at plough,
    Robert's kin, and John's, and Ned's,
And the Squire, and Lady Susan, murmur mildly
      to me now.

I saw him steal the light away
  That haunted in her eye :
It went so gently none could say
More than that it was there one day
  And missing by-and-by.

I watched her longer, and he stole
  Her lily tincts and rose ;
All her young sprightliness of soul
Next fell beneath his cold control,
  And disappeared like those.

I asked : " Why do you serve her so ?
  Do you, for some glad day,
Hoard these her sweets — ? " He said, " O no,
They charm not me ; I bid Time throw
  Them carelessly away."

Said I : " We call that cruelty —
  We, your poor mortal kind."
He mused. " The thought is new to me.
Forsooth, though I men's master be,
  Theirs is the teaching mind ! "

GOD-FORGOTTEN

I TOWERED far, and lo! I stood within
　The presence of the Lord Most High,
Sent thither by the sons of Earth, to win
　　　Some answer to their cry.

— " The Earth, sayest thou? The Human race?
　By Me created? Sad its lot?
Nay: I have no remembrance of such place:
　　　Such world I fashioned not." —

— " O Lord, forgive me when I say
　Thou spakest the word that made it all." —
" The Earth of men — let me bethink me. . . .
　　Yea!
　　　　I dimly do recall

" Some tiny sphere I built long back
　(Mid millions of such shapes of mine)
So named. . . . It perished, surely — not a wrack
　　　Remaining, or a sign?

" It lost my interest from the first,
　My aims therefor succeeding ill;
Haply it died of doing as it durst?" —
　　　" Lord, it existeth still." —

" Dark, then, its life! For not a cry
　Of aught it bears do I now hear;
Of its own act the threads were snapt whereby
　　　Its plaints had reached mine ear.

113

"It used to ask for gifts of good,
Till came its severance, self-entailed,
When sudden silence on that side ensued,
    And has till now prevailed.

"All other orbs have kept in touch;
Their voicings reach me speedily:
Thy people took upon them overmuch
    In sundering them from me!

"And it is strange — though sad enough —
Earth's race should think that one whose call
Frames, daily, shining spheres of flawless stuff
    Must heed their tainted ball! . . .

"But sayest it is by pangs distraught,
And strife, and silent suffering? —
Sore grieved am I that injury should be wrought
    Even on so poor a thing!

"Thou shouldst have learnt that *Not to Mend*
For Me could mean but *Not to Know*:
Hence, Messengers! and straightway put an end
    To what men undergo." . . .

Homing at dawn, I thought to see
One of the Messengers standing by.
 Oh, childish thought! . . . Yet often it comes
  to me
    When trouble hovers nigh.

" I HAVE finished another year," said God,
    " In grey, green, white, and brown ;
I have strewn the leaf upon the sod,
Sealed up the worm within the clod,
    And let the last sun down."

" And what's the good of it ? " I said,
    " What reasons made you call
From formless void this earth we tread,
When nine-and-ninety can be read
    Why nought should be at all ?

" Yea, Sire ; why shaped you us, ' who in
    This tabernacle groan ' —
If ever a joy be found herein,
Such joy no man had wished to win
    If he had never known ! "

Then he : " My labours — logicless —
    You may explain ; not I :
Sense-sealed I have wrought, without a guess
That I evolved a Consciousness
    To ask for reasons why.

" Strange that ephemeral creatures who
    By my own ordering are,
Should see the shortness of my view,
Use ethic tests I never knew,
    Or made provision for ! "

He sank to raptness as of yore,
　　And opening New Year's Day
Wove it by rote as theretofore,
And went on working evermore
　　In his unweeting way.

THE INTERLOPER

" And I saw the figure and visage of Madness seeking for a home."

THERE are three folk driving in a quaint old chaise,
And the cliff-side track looks green and fair ;
I view them talking in quiet glee
As they drop down towards the puffins' lair
      By the roughest of ways ;
But another with the three rides on, I see,
      Whom I like not to be there !

No : it's not anybody you think of. Next
A dwelling appears by a slow sweet stream
Where two sit happy and half in the dark :
They read, helped out by a frail-wick'd gleam,
      Some rhythmic text ;
But one sits with them whom they don't mark,
      One I'm wishing could not be there.

No : not whom you knew and name. And now
I discern gay diners in a mansion-place,
And the guests dropping wit — pert, prim, or
    choice,
And the hostess's tender and laughing face,
      And the host's bland brow ;
But I cannot help hearing a hollow voice,
      And I'd fain not hear it there.

No : it's not from the stranger you met once. Ah,
Yet a goodlier scene than that succeeds ;
People on a lawn — quite a crowd of them. Yes,
And they chatter and ramble as fancy leads ;
      And they say, " Hurrah ! "

To a blithe speech made ; save one, mirthless,
        Who ought not to be there.

Nay : it's not the pale Form your imagings raise,
That waits on us all at a destined time,
It is not the Fourth Figure the Furnace showed ;
O that it were such a shape sublime
        In these latter days !
It is that under which best lives corrode ;
        Would, would it could not be there !

WAGTAIL AND BABY

A BABY watched a ford, whereto
    A wagtail came for drinking;
A blaring bull went wading through,
    The wagtail showed no shrinking.

A stallion splashed his way across,
    The birdie nearly sinking;
He gave his plumes a twitch and toss,
    And held his own unblinking.

Next saw the baby round the spot
    A mongrel slowly slinking;
The wagtail gazed, but faltered not
    In dip and sip and prinking.

A perfect gentleman then neared;
    The wagtail, in a winking,
With terror rose and disappeared;
    The baby fell a-thinking.

THE GLIMPSE

She sped through the door
And, following in haste,
And stirred to the core,
I entered hot-faced ;
But I could not find her,
No sign was behind her.
" Where is she ? " I said :
— " Who ? " they asked that sat there ;
" Not a soul's come in sight."
— " A maid with red hair."
— " Ah." They paled. " She is dead.
People see her at night,
But you are the first
On whom she has burst
In the keen common light."

It was ages ago,
When I was quite strong :
I have waited since, — O,
I have waited so long !
— Yea, I set me to own
The house, where now lone
I dwell in void rooms
Booming hollow as tombs !
But I never come near her,
Though nightly I hear her.
And my cheek has grown thin
And my hair has grown gray
With this waiting therein ;
But she still keeps away !

"I LOOK INTO MY GLASS"

I LOOK into my glass,
And view my wasting skin,
And say, " Would God it came to pass
My heart had shrunk as thin ! "

For then, I, undistrest
By hearts grown cold to me,
Could lonely wait my endless rest
With equanimity.

But Time, to make me grieve,
Part steals, lets part abide ;
And shakes this fragile frame at eve
With throbbings of noontide.

WHY did you give no hint that night
That quickly after the morrow's dawn,
And calmly, as if indifferent quite,
You would close your term here, up and be gone
      Where I could not follow
      With wing of swallow
To gain one glimpse of you ever anon !

      Never to bid good-bye,
      Or lip me the softest call,
Or utter a wish for a word, while I
Saw morning harden upon the wall,
      Unmoved, unknowing
      That your great going
Had place that moment, and altered all.

Why do you make me leave the house
And think for a breath it is you I see
At the end of the alley of bending boughs
Where so often at dusk you used to be ;
      Till in darkening darkness
      The yawning blankness
Of the perspective sickens me !

      You were she who abode
      By those red-veined rocks far West,
You were the swan-necked one who rode
Along the beetling Beeny Crest,
      And, reining nigh me,
      Would muse and eye me,
While Life unrolled us its very best.

Why, then, latterly did we not speak,
Did we not think of those days long dead,
And ere your vanishing strive to seek
That time's renewal ? We might have said,
    " In this bright spring weather
    We'll visit together
Those places that once we visited."

    Well, well ! All's past amend,
    Unchangeable.   It must go.
I seem but a dead man held on end
To sink down soon. . . . O you could not know
    That such swift fleeing
    No soul foreseeing —
Not even I — would undo me so !

December 1912

WE went a day's excursion to the stream,
Basked by the bank, and bent to the ripplegleam,
     And I did not know
     That life would show,
However it might flower, no finer glow.

I walked in the Sunday sunshine by the road
That wound towards the wicket of your abode,
     And I did not think
     That life would shrink
To nothing ere it shed a rosier pink.

Unlooked for I arrived on a rainy night,
And you hailed me at the door by the swaying light,
     And I full forgot
     That life might not
Again be touching that ecstatic height.

And that calm eve when you walked up the stair,
After a gaiety prolonged and rare,
     No thought soever
     That you might never
Walk down again, struck me as I stood there.

RAIN ON A GRAVE

Clouds spout upon her
   Their waters amain
   In ruthless disdain, —
Her who but lately
   Had shivered with pain
As at touch of dishonour
If there had lit on her
So coldly, so straightly,
   Such arrows of rain:

One who to shelter
   Her delicate head
Would quicken and quicken
   Each tentative tread
If drops chanced to pelt her
   That summertime spills
   In dust-paven rills
When thunder-clouds thicken
   And birds close their bills.

Would that I lay there
   And she were housed here!
Or better, together
Were folded away there
Exposed to one weather
We both, — who would stray there
When sunny the day there
   Or evening was clear
   At the prime of the year.

Soon will be growing
   Green blades from her mound,
And daisies be showing
   Like stars on the ground,·
Till she form part of them —
Ay — the sweet heart of them,
Loved beyond measure
With a child's pleasure
   All her life's round.

   Jan. 31, 1913

A DREAM OR NO

WHY go to Saint-Juliot? What's Juliot to me?
  Some strange necromancy
  But charmed me to fancy
That much of my life claims the spot as its key.

Yes. I have had dreams of that place in the West,
  And a maiden abiding
  Thereat as in hiding;
Fair-eyed and white-shouldered, broad-browed and
  brown-tressed.

And of how, coastward bound on a night long ago,
  There lonely I found her,
  The sea-birds around her,
And other than nigh things uncaring to know.

So sweet her life there (in my thought has it seemed)
  That quickly she drew me
  To take her unto me,
And lodge her long years with me. Such have I
  dreamed.

But nought of that maid from Saint-Juliot I see;
  Can she ever have been here,
  And shed her life's sheen here,
The woman I thought a long housemate with me?

Does there even a place like Saint-Juliot exist?
  Or a Valency Valley
  With stream and leafed alley,
Or Beeny, or Bos with its flounce flinging mist?

February 1913

BEENY did not quiver,
   Juliot grew not gray,
Thin Vallency's river
   Held its wonted way.
Bos seemed not to utter
   Dimmest note of dirge,
Targan mouth a mutter
   To its creamy surge.

Yet though these, unheeding,
   Listless, passed the hour
Of her spirit's speeding,
   She had, in her flower,
Sought and loved the places —
   Much and often pined
For their lonely faces
   When in towns confined.

Why did not Vallency
   In his purl deplore
One whose haunts were whence he
   Drew his limpid store?
Why did Bos not thunder,
   Targan apprehend
Body and Breath were sunder
   Of their former friend?

"I FOUND HER OUT THERE"

I FOUND her out there
On a slope few see,
That falls westwardly
To the salt-edged air,
Where the ocean breaks
On the purple strand,
And the hurricane shakes
The solid land.

I brought her here,
And have laid her to rest
In a noiseless nest
No sea beats near.
She will never be stirred
In her loamy cell
By the waves long heard
And loved so well.

So she does not sleep
By those haunted heights
The Atlantic smites
And the blind gales sweep,
Whence she often would gaze
At Dundagel's famed head,
While the dipping blaze
Dyed her face fire-red ;

And would sigh at the tale
Of sunk Lyonnesse,
As a wind-tugged tress
Flapped her cheek like a flail ;

Or listen at whiles
With a thought-bound brow
To the murmuring miles
She is far from now.

Yet her shade, maybe,
Will creep underground
Till it catch the sound
Of that western sea
As it swells and sobs
Where she once domiciled,
And joy in its throbs
With the heart of a child.

BEENY CLIFF

March 1870 — March 1913

I

O THE opal and the sapphire of that wandering
  western sea,
And the woman riding high above with bright hair
  flapping free —
The woman whom I loved so, and who loyally
  loved me.

II

The pale mews plained below us, and the waves
  seemed far away
In a nether sky, engrossed in saying their ceaseless
  babbling say,
As we laughed light-heartedly aloft on that clear-
  sunned March day.

III

A little cloud then cloaked us, and there flew an
  irised rain,
And the Atlantic dyed its levels with a dull mis-
  featured stain,
And then the sun burst out again, and purples
  prinked the main.

IV

— Still in all its chasmal beauty bulks old Beeny to
  the sky,
And shall she and I not go there once again now
  March is nigh,
And the sweet things said in that March say anew
  there by and by ?

V

What if still in chasmal beauty looms that wild weird
    western shore,
The woman now is — elsewhere — whom the
    ambling pony bore,
And nor knows nor cares for Beeny, and will laugh
    there nevermore.

THE PHANTOM HORSEWOMAN

I

QUEER are the ways of a man I know:
  He comes and stands
  In a careworn craze,
  And looks at the sands
  And the seaward haze
  With moveless hands
  And face and gaze,
  Then turns to go . . .
And what does he see when he gazes so?

II

They say he sees as an instant thing
  More clear than to-day,
  A sweet soft scene
  That was once in play
  By that briny green;
  Yes, notes alway
  Warm, real, and keen,
  What his back years bring —
A phantom of his own figuring.

III

Of this vision of his they might say more:
  Not only there
  Does he see this sight,
  But everywhere
  In his brain — day, night,

As if on the air
It were drawn rose-bright —
Yea, far from that shore
Does he carry this vision of heretofore :

IV

A ghost-girl-rider.   And though, toil-tried,
He withers daily,
Time touches her not,
But she still rides gaily
In his rapt thought
On that shagged and shaly
Atlantic spot,
And as when first eyed
Draws rein and sings to the swing of the tide.

1913

THE CLOCK OF THE YEARS

"A spirit passed before my face; the hair of my flesh stood up."

AND the Spirit said,
" I can make the clock of the years go backward,
But am loth to stop it where you will."
    And I cried, " Agreed
    To that. Proceed :
    It's better than dead ! "

    He answered, " Peace " ;
And called her up — as last before me ;
Then younger, younger she freshed, to the year
    I first had known
    Her woman-grown,
    And I cried, " Cease ! —

    " Thus far is good —
It is enough — let her stay thus always ! "
But alas for me — He shook his head :
    No stop was there ;
    And she waned child-fair,
    And to babyhood.

    Still less in mien
To my great sorrow became she slowly,
And smalled till she was nought at all
    In his checkless griff ;
    And it was as if
    She had never been.

       " Better," I plained,
" She were dead as before ! The memory of her
Had lived in me ; but it cannot now ! "
       And coldly his voice :
       " It was your choice
       To mar the ordained."

HIS COUNTRY

I JOURNEYED from my native spot
    Across the south sea shine,
And found that people in hall and cot
Laboured and suffered each his lot
    Even as I did mine.

Thus noting them in meads and marts
    It did not seem to me
That my dear country with its hearts,
Minds, yearnings, worse and better parts
    Had ended with the sea.

I further and further went anon,
    As such I still surveyed,
And further yet — yea, on and on,
And all the men I looked upon
    Had heart-strings fellow-made.

I traced the whole terrestrial round,
    Homing the other side ;
Then said I, " What is there to bound
My denizenship ? It seems I have found
    Its scope to be world-wide."

I asked me : " Whom have I to fight,
    And whom have I to dare,
And whom to weaken, crush, and blight ?
My country seems to have kept in sight
    On my way everywhere."

1913

EPEISODIA

I

Past the hills that peep
Where the leaze is smiling,
On and on beguiling
Crisply-cropping sheep;
Under boughs of brushwood
Linking tree and tree
In a shade of lushwood,
    There caressed we!

II

Hemmed by city walls
That outshut the sunlight,
In a foggy dun light,
Where the footstep falls
With a pit-pat wearisome
In its cadency
On the flagstones drearisome,
    There pressed we!

III

Where in wild-winged crowds
Blown birds show their whiteness
Up against the lightness
Of the clammy clouds;
By the random river
Pushing to the sea,
Under bents that quiver,
    There shall rest we!

LAST WORDS TO A DUMB FRIEND

Pet was never mourned as you,
Purrer of the spotless hue,
Plumy tail, and wistful gaze
While you humoured our queer ways,
Or outshrilled your morning call
Up the stairs and through the hall —
Foot suspended in its fall —
While, expectant, you would stand
Arched, to meet the stroking hand ;
Till your way you chose to wend
Yonder, to your tragic end.

Never another pet for me !
Let your place all vacant be ;
Better blankness day by day
Than companion torn away.
Better bid his memory fade,
Better blot each mark he made,
Selfishly escape distress
By contrived forgetfulness,
Than preserve his prints to make
Every morn and eve an ache.

From the chair whereon he sat
Sweep his fur, nor wince thereat ;
Rake his little pathways out
Mid the bushes roundabout ;
Smooth away his talons' mark
From the claw-worn pine-tree bark,
Where he climbed as dusk embrowned,
Waiting us who loitered round.

Strange it is this speechless thing,
Subject to our mastering,
Subject for his life and food
To our gift, and time, and mood;
Timid pensioner of us Powers,
His existence ruled by ours,
Should — by crossing at a breath
Into safe and shielded death,
By the merely taking hence
Of his insignificance —
Loom as largened to the sense,
Shape as part, above man's will,
Of the Imperturbable.

As a prisoner, flight debarred,
Exercising in a yard,
Still retain I, troubled, shaken,
Mean estate, by him forsaken;
And this home, which scarcely took
Impress from his little look,
By his faring to the Dim
Grows all eloquent of him.

Housemate, I can think you still
Bounding to the window-sill,
Over which I vaguely see
Your small mound beneath the tree,
Showing in the autumn shade
That you moulder where you played.

AN ANCIENT TO ANCIENTS

WHERE once we danced, where once we sang,
   Gentlemen,
The floors are sunken, cobwebs hang,
And cracks creep ; worms have fed upon
The doors.   Yea, sprightlier times were then
Than now, with harps and tabrets gone,
   Gentlemen !

Where once we rowed, where once we sailed,
   Gentlemen,
And damsels took the tiller, veiled
Against too strong a stare (God wot
Their fancy, then or anywhen !)
Upon that shore we are clean forgot,
   Gentlemen !

We have lost somewhat, afar and near,
   Gentlemen,
The thinning of our ranks each year
Affords a hint we are nigh undone,
That we shall not be ever again
The marked of many, loved of one,
   Gentlemen.

In dance the polka hit our wish,
   Gentlemen,
The paced quadrille, the spry schottische,
" Sir Roger ". — And in opera spheres
The " Girl " (the famed " Bohemian "),
And " Trovatore ", held the ears,
   Gentlemen.

·This season's paintings do not please,
        Gentlemen,
Like Etty, Mulready, Maclise ;
Throbbing romance has waned and wanned ;
No wizard wields the witching pen
Of Bulwer, Scott, Dumas, and Sand,
        Gentlemen.

The bower we shrined to Tennyson,
        Gentlemen,
Is roof-wrecked ; damps there drip upon
Sagged seats, the creeper-nails are rust,
The spider is sole denizen ;
Even she who voiced those rhymes is dust,
        Gentlemen !

We who met sunrise sanguine-souled,
        Gentlemen,
Are wearing weary. We are old ;
These younger press ; we feel our rout
Is imminent to Aïdes' den, —
That evening shades are stretching out,
        Gentlemen !

And yet, though ours be failing frames,
        Gentlemen,
So were some others' history names,
Who trode their track light-limbed and fast
As these youth, and not alien
From enterprise, to their long last,
        Gentlemen.

-Sophocles, Plato, Socrates,
         Gentlemen,
Pythagoras, Thucydides,
Herodotus, and Homer, — yea,
Clement, Augustine, Origen,
Burnt brightlier towards their setting-day,
         Gentlemen.

And ye, red-lipped and smooth-browed; list,
         Gentlemen;
Much is there waits you we have missed;
Much lore we leave you worth the knowing,
Much, much has lain outside our ken:
Nay, rush not: time serves: we are going,
         Gentlemen.

You, Morningtide Star, now are steady-eyed, over
    the east,
      I know it as if I saw you ;
You, Beeches, engrave on the sky your thin twigs,
    even the least ;
      Had I paper and pencil I'd draw you.

You, Meadow, are white with your counterpane
    cover of dew,
      I see it as if I were there ;
You, Churchyard, are lightening faint from the
    shade of the yew,
      The names creeping out everywhere.

SO VARIOUS

You may have met a man — quite young —
A brisk-eyed youth, and highly strung :
        One whose desires
        And inner fires
        Moved him as wires.

And you may have met one stiff and old,
If not in years ; of manner cold ;
        Who seemed as stone,
        And never had known
        Of mirth or moan.

And there may have crossed your path a lover,
In whose clear depths you could discover
        A staunch, robust,
        And tender trust,
        Through storm and gust.

And you may have also known one fickle,
Whose fancies changed as the silver sickle
        Of yonder moon,
        Which shapes so soon
        To demilune !

You entertained a person once
Whom you internally deemed a dunce :—
        As he sat in view
        Just facing you
        You saw him through.

You came to know a learned seer
Of whom you read the surface mere :
        Your soul quite sank ;
        Brain of such rank
        Dubbed yours a blank.

Anon you quizzed a man of sadness,
Who never could have known true gladness :
        Just for a whim
        You pitied him
        In his sore trim.

You journeyed with a man so glad
You never could conceive him sad :
        He proved to be
        Indubitably
        Good company.

You lit on an unadventurous slow man,
Who, said you, need be feared by no man ;
        That his slack deeds
        And sloth must needs
        Produce but weeds.

A man of enterprise, shrewd and swift,
Who never suffered affairs to drift,
        You eyed for a time
        Just in his prime,
        And judged he might climb.

You smoked beside one who forgot
All that you said, or grasped it not.

Quite a poor thing,
Not worth a sting
By satirizing !

Next year you nearly lost for ever
Goodwill from one who forgot slights never ;
    And, with unease,
    Felt you must seize
    Occasion to please . . .

Now. . . . All these specimens of man,
So various in their pith and plan,
    Curious to say
    Were *one* man.   Yea,
    I was all they.

GEORGE MEREDITH

(1828–1909)

FORTY years back, when much had place
That since has perished out of mind,
I heard that voice and saw that face.

He spoke as one afoot will wind
A morning horn ere men awake ;
His note was trenchant, turning kind.

He was of those whose wit can shake
And riddle to the very core
The counterfeits that Time will break.

Of late, when we two met once more,
The luminous countenance and rare
Shone just as forty years before.

So that, when now all tongues declare
His shape unseen by his green hill,
I scarce believe he sits not there.

No matter. Further and further still
Through the world's vaporous vitiate air
His words wing on — as live words will.

CHILDHOOD AMONG THE FERNS

I SAT one sprinkling day upon the lea,
Where tall-stemmed ferns spread out luxuriantly,
And nothing but those tall ferns sheltered me.

The rain gained strength, and damped each lopping
    frond,
Ran down their stalks beside me and beyond,
And shaped slow-creeping rivulets as I conned,

With pride, my spray-roofed house. And though
    anon
Some drops pierced its green rafters, I sat on,
Making pretence I was not rained upon.

The sun then burst, and brought forth a sweet
    breath
From the limp ferns as they dried underneath:
I said: "I could live on here thus till death";

And queried in the green rays as I sate:
"Why should I have to grow to man's estate,
And this afar-noised World perambulate?"

COOMB-FIRTREES say that Life is a moan,
    And Clyffe-hill Clump says "Yea!"
But Yell'ham says a thing of its own:
      It's not "Gray, gray
      Is Life alway!"
    That Yell'ham says,
Nor that Life is for ends unknown.

It says that Life would signify
    A thwarted purposing:
That we come to live, and are called to die.
      Yes, that's the thing
      In fall, in spring,
    That Yell'ham says: —
"Life offers — to deny!"

HE NEVER EXPECTED MUCH

[or]

A CONSIDERATION

[*A reflection*] on my Eighty-sixth Birthday

WELL, World, you have kept faith with me,
   Kept faith with me ;
Upon the whole you have proved to be
   Much as you said you were.
Since as a child I used to lie
Upon the leaze and watch the sky,
Never, I own, expected I
   That life would all be fair.

'Twas then you said, and since have said,
   Times since have said,
In that mysterious voice you shed
   From clouds and hills around :
" Many have loved me desperately,
Many with smooth serenity,
While some have shown contempt of me
   Till they dropped underground.

" I do not promise overmuch,
   Child ; overmuch ;
Just neutral-tinted haps and such,"
   You said to minds like mine.
Wise warning for your credit's sake !
Which I for one failed not to take,
And hence could stem such strain and ache
   As each year might assign.

FROM "THE DYNASTS"

PROLOGUE

SHADE OF THE EARTH

What of the Immanent Will and Its designs?

SPIRIT OF THE YEARS

It works unconsciously, as heretofore,
Eternal artistries in Circumstance,
Whose patterns, wrought by rapt æsthetic rote,
Seem in themselves Its single listless aim,
And not their consequence.

CHORUS OF THE PITIES
(aerial music)

Still thus? Still thus?
Ever unconscious!
An automatic sense
Unweeting why or whence?
Be, then, the inevitable, as of old,
Although that so it be we dare not hold!

SPIRIT OF THE YEARS

Hold what ye list, fond unbelieving Sprites,
You cannot swerve the pulsion of the Byss,
Which thinking on, yet weighing not Its thought,
Unchecks Its clock-like laws.

SPIRIT SINISTER
(aside)

Good, as before,
My little engines, then, will still have play.

SPIRIT OF THE PITIES

Why doth It so and so, and ever so,
This viewless, voiceless Turner of the Wheel?

SPIRIT OF THE YEARS

As one sad story runs, It lends Its heed
To other worlds, being wearied out with this ;
Wherefore Its mindlessness of earthly woes.
Some, too, have told at whiles that rightfully
Its warefulness, Its care, this planet lost
When in her early growth and crudity
By bad mad acts of severance men contrived,
Working such nescience by their own device. —
Yea, so it stands in certain chronicles,
Though not in mine.

SPIRIT OF THE PITIES

       Meet is it, none the less,
To bear in thought that though Its consciousness
May be estranged, engrossed afar, or sealed,
Sublunar shocks may wake Its watch anon?

SPIRIT OF THE YEARS

Nay. In the Foretime, even to the germ of Being,
Nothing appears of shape to indicate
That cognizance has marshalled things terrene,
Or will (such is my thinking) in my span.
Rather they show that, like a knitter drowsed,
Whose fingers play in skilled unmindfulness,
The Will has woven with an absent heed
Since life first was ; and ever will so weave.

1805

RECORDING ANGEL

(from a book, in recitative)

Now mellow-eyed Peace is made captive,
    And Vengeance is chartered
To deal forth its dooms on the Peoples
    With sword and with spear.

Men's musings are busy with forecasts
    Of musters and battle,
And visions of shock and disaster
    Rise red on the year.

The easternmost ruler sits wistful,
    And tense he to midward;
The King to the west mans his borders
    In front and in rear.

While one they eye, flushed from his crowning,
    Ranks legions around him
To shake the enisled neighbour nation
    And close her career!

SEMICHORUS I OF RUMOURS

(aerial music)

O woven-winged squadrons of Toulon
    And fellows of Rochefort,
Wait, wait for a wind, and draw westward
    Ere Nelson be near!

For he reads not your force, or your freightage
    Of warriors fell-handed,
Or when they will join for the onset,
    Or whither they steer !

SEMICHORUS II

O Nelson, so zealous a watcher
    Through months-long of cruizing,
Thy foes may elude thee a moment,
    Put forth, and get clear ;

And rendezvous westerly straightway
    With Spain's aiding navies,
And hasten to head violation
    Of Albion's frontier !

NELSON

In short, dear Coll, the letter which you wrote me
Had so much pith that I was fain to see you ;
For I am sure that you indeed divine
The true intent and compass of a plot
Which I have spelled in vain.

COLLINGWOOD

                I weighed it thus :
Their flight to the Indies being to draw us off,
That and no more, and clear these coasts of us —
The standing obstacle to his device —
He cared not what was done at Martinique,
Or where, provided that the general end
Should not be jeopardized — that is to say,
The full-united squadron's quick return. —
Gravina and Vill'neuve, once back to Europe,
Can straight make Ferrol, raise there the blockade,
Then haste to Brest, there to relieve Ganteaume,
And next with four- or five-and-fifty sail
Bear down upon our coast as they see fit. —
I read they aim to strike at Ireland still,
As formerly, and as I wrote to you.

NELSON

So far your thoughtful and sagacious words
Have hit the facts. But 'tis no Irish bay
The villains aim to drop their anchors in ;
My word for it : they make the Wessex shore,

N   159

And this vast squadron handled by Vill'neuve
Is meant to cloak the passage of their strength,
Massed in those transports — we being kept else-
    where
By feigning forces. — Good God, Collingwood,
I must be gone ! Yet two more days remain
Ere I can get away. — I must be gone !

COLLINGWOOD

Wherever you may go to, my dear lord,
You carry victory with you. Let them launch,
Your name will blow them back, as sou'-west gales
The gulls that beat against them from the shore.

NELSON

Good Collingwood, I know you trust in me ;
But ships are ships, and do not kindly come
Out of the slow docks of the Admiralty
Like wharfside pigeons when they are whistled
    for : —
And there's a damned disparity of force,
Which means tough work awhile for you and me !

(*The Spirit of the Years whispers to* NELSON)

And I have warnings, warnings, Collingwood,
That my effective hours are shortening here ;
Strange warnings now and then, as 'twere within me
Which, though I fear them not, I recognize ! . . .
However, by God's help, I'll live to meet
These foreign boasters ; yea, I'll finish them ;
And then — well, Gunner Death may finish me !

View not your life so gloomily, my lord:
One charmed, a needed purpose to fulfil!

Ah, Coll. Lead bullets are not all that wound. . . .
I have a feeling here of dying fires,
A sense of strong and deep unworded censure,
Which, compassing about my private life,
Makes all my public service lustreless
In my own eyes. — I fear I am much condemned
For those dear Naples and Palermo days,
And her who was the sunshine of them all! . . .
He who is with himself dissatisfied,
Though all the world find satisfaction in him,
Is like a rainbow-coloured bird gone blind,
That gives delight it shares not. Happiness?
It's the philosopher's stone no alchemy
Shall light on in this world I am weary of. —
Smiling I'd pass to my long home to-morrow
Could I with honour, and my country's gain.
— But let's adjourn. I waste your hours ashore
By such ill-timed confessions!

KING

YES, yes ; I grasp your reasons, Mr. Pitt,
And grant you audience gladly.   More than that,
Your visit to this shore is apt and timely,
And if it do but yield you needful rest
From fierce debate, and other strains of office
Which you and I in common have to bear,
'Twill be well earned.   The bathing is unmatched
Elsewhere in Europe, — see its mark on me !
The air like liquid life. — But of this matter :
What argue these late movements seen abroad ?
What of the country now the session's past ;
What of the country, eh ? and of the war ?

PITT

The thoughts I have laid before your Majesty
Would make for this, in sum : —
That Mr. Fox, Lord Grenville, and their friends,
Be straightway asked to join.   With Melville gone,
With Sidmouth, and with Buckinghamshire too,
The steerage of affairs has stood of late
Somewhat provisional, as you, sir, know,
With stop-gap functions thrust on offices
Which common weal can tolerate but awhile.
So, for the weighty reasons I have urged,
I do repeat my most respectful hope
To win your Majesty's ungrudged assent
To what I have proposed.

KING

But nothing, sure,

Has been more plain to all, dear Mr. Pitt,
Than that your own proved energy and scope
Is ample, without aid, to carry on
Our just crusade against this Corsican.
Why, then, go calling Fox and Grenville in?
Such helps we need not. Pray you think upon't,
And speak to me again. — We've had alarms
Making us skip like crackers at our heels,
That Bonaparte had landed close hereby.

PITT

Such rumours come as regularly as harvest.

KING

And now he has left Boulogne with all his host?
Was it his object to invade at all,
Or was his vast assemblage there a blind?

PITT

Undoubtedly he meant invasion, sir,
Had fortune favoured. He may try it yet.
And, as I said, could we but close with Fox——

KING

But, but; — I ask, what is his object now?
Lord Nelson's Captain — Hardy — whose old home
Stands in a peaceful vale hard by us here —
Who came two weeks ago to see his friends,
I talked to in this room a lengthy while.
He says our navy still is in thick night
As to the aims by sea of Bonaparte

163

Now the Boulogne attempt has fizzled out,
And what he schemes afloat with Spain combined.
The " Victory " lay that fortnight at Spithead,
And Nelson since has gone aboard and sailed ;
Yes, sailed again.   The " Royal Sovereign " follows,
And others her.   Nelson was hailed and cheered
To huskiness while leaving Southsea shore,
Gentle and simple wildly thronging round.

PITT

Ay, sir.   Young women hung upon his arm,
And old ones blessed, and stroked him with their
    hands.

KING

Ah — you have heard, of course.   God speed him,
    Pitt.

PITT

Amen, amen !

KING

                I read it as a thing
Of signal augury, and one which bodes
Heaven's confidence in me and in my line,
That I should rule as King in such an age ! . . .

AFTER TRAFALGAR

PITT

(*standing up after repeated calls*)

My lords and gentlemen : — You have toasted me
As one who has saved England and her cause.
I thank you, gentlemen, unfeignedly.
But — no man has saved England, let me say :
England has saved herself, by her exertions :
She will, I trust, save Europe by her example !

> (*Loud applause, during which he sits down, rises, and sits
> down again. The scene then shuts, and the night without
> has place*)

SPIRIT OF THE YEARS

*Those words of this man Pitt — his last large words,
As I may prophesy — that ring to-night
In their first mintage to the feasters here,
Will spread with ageing, lodge, and crystallize,
And stand embedded in the English tongue
Till it grow thin, outworn, and cease to be. —
So is't ordained by That Which all ordains ;
For words were never winged with apter grace,
Or blent with happier choice of time and place,
To hold the imagination of this strenuous race.*

THE BOATMAN'S SONG

THE NIGHT OF TRAFALGAR

I

In the wild October night-time, when the wind
        raved round the land,
And the Back-sea [1] met the Front-sea, and our doors
        were blocked with sand,
And we heard the drub of Dead-man's Bay, where
        bones of thousands are,
We knew not what the day had done for us at Tra-
        falgár.
                (All) Had done,
                        Had done,
                For us at Trafalgár!

II

" Pull hard, and make the Nothe, or down we go ! "
        one says, says he.
We pulled ; and bedtime brought the storm ; but
        snug at home slept we.
Yet all the while our gallants after fighting through
        the day,
Were beating up and down the dark, sou'-west of
        Cadiz Bay.
                The dark,
                The dark,
                Sou'-west of Cadiz Bay !

---

[1] In those days the hind-part of the harbour adjoining this
scene was so named, and at high tides the waves washed across
the isthmus at a point called " The Narrows."

The victors and the vanquished then the storm it
     tossed and tore,
As hard they strove, those worn-out men, upon that
     surly shore ;
Dead Nelson and his half-dead crew, his foes from
     near and far,
Were rolled together on the deep that night at
     Trafalgár !

            The deep,
            The deep,
        That night at Trafalgár !

AFTER AUSTERLITZ

SHOCKERWICK HOUSE, NEAR BATH

The interior of the Picture Gallery. Enter WILTSHIRE *the owner, and* PITT, *who looks emaciated and walks feebly.*

WILTSHIRE

(pointing to a portrait)

Now here you have the lady we discussed :
A fine example of his manner, sir ?

PITT

It is a fine example, sir, indeed, —
With that transparency amid the shades,
And those thin blue-green-greyish leafages
Behind the pillar in the background there,
Which seem the leaves themselves. — Ah, this is
    Quin.

(Moving to another picture)

WILTSHIRE

Yes, Quin. A man of varied parts, though rough
And choleric at times. Yet, at his best,
As Falstaff, never matched, they say. But I
Had not the fate to see him in the flesh.

PITT

Churchill well carves him in his " Characters " : —
" His eyes, in gloomy socket taught to roll,
Proclaimed the sullen habit of his soul.
In fancied scenes, as in Life's real plan,
He could not for a moment sink the man :

Nature, in spite of all his skill, crept in ;
Horatio, Dorax, Falstaff — still 'twas Quin."
— He was at Bath when Gainsborough settled
    there
In that house in the Circus which we know. —
I like the portrait much. — The brilliancy
Of Gainsborough lies in this his double sway ;
Sovereign of landscape he ; of portraiture
Joint monarch with Sir Joshua. . . . Ah ? — that's
    — hark !
Is that the patter of a horse's hoofs
Along the road ?

WILTSHIRE

               I notice nothing, sir.

PITT

It is a gallop, growing quite distinct.
And — can it be a messenger for me !

WILTSHIRE

I hope no ugly European news
To stop the honour of this visit, sir !

> (*They listen. The gallop of the horse grows louder, and is
> checked at the door of the house. There is a hasty
> knocking, and a courier, splashed with mud from hard
> riding, is shown into the gallery. He presents a dispatch
> to* PITT, *who sits down and hurriedly opens it*)

PITT

(to himself)

O heavy news indeed ! . . . Disastrous ; dire !

(He appears overcome as he sits, and covers his forehead with his hand)

169

I trust you are not ill, sir?

(after some moments)

                 Could I have
A little brandy, sir, quick brought to me?

In one brief minute.
       (Brandy is brought in, and PITT *takes it)*

Now leave me, please, alone. I'll call anon.
Is there a map of Europe handy here?

> (WILTSHIRE *fetches a map from the library, and spreads it
> before the minister.* WILTSHIRE, *courier, and servant
> go out)*

O God that I should live to see this day!

> *(He remains awhile in a profound reverie; then resumes the
> reading of the dispatch)*

" Defeated — the Allies — quite overthrown
At Austerlitz — last week." — Where's Austerlitz?
— But what avails it where the place is now;
What corpse is curious on the longitude
And situation of his cemetery! . . .
The Austrians and the Russians overcome,
That vast adventuring army is set free
To bend unhindered strength against our strand. . . .
So do my plans through all these plodding years

Announce them built in vain!
His heel on Europe, monarchies in chains
To France, I am as though I had never been!

> (*He gloomily ponders the dispatch and the map some minutes longer. At last he rises with difficulty, and rings the bell. A servant enters*)

Call up my carriage, please you, now at once;
And tell your master I return to Bath
This moment — I may want a little help
In getting to the door here.

SERVANT

                Sir, I will,
And summon you my master instantly.

> (*He goes out and re-enters with* WILTSHIRE. PITT *is assisted from the room*)

PITT

Roll up that map. 'Twill not be needed now
These ten years! Realms, laws, peoples, dynasties,
Are churning to a pulp within the maw
Of empire-making Lust and personal Gain!

> (*Exeunt* PITT, WILTSHIRE, *and servant; and in a few minutes the carriage is heard driving off, and the scene closes*)

NAPOLEON AND FOX

SPIRIT OF THE PITIES

What mean these couriers shooting shuttlewise
To Paris and to London, turn and turn?

RUMOURS

(chanting in antiphons)

I

The aforesaid tidings from the minister, spokesman in
England's cause to states afar,

II

Traverse the waters borne by one of such ; and thereto
Bonaparte's responses are :

I

" The principles of honour and of truth which ever
actuate the sender's mind

II

" Herein are written largely ! Take our thanks : we
read that this conjuncture undesigned

I

" Unfolds felicitous means of showing you that still our
eyes are set, as yours, on peace,

*" To which great end the Treaty of Amiens must be the
    groundwork of our amities."*

I

*From London then : " The path to amity the King of
    England studies to pursue ;*

II

*" With Russia hand in hand he is yours to close the long
    convulsions thrilling Europe through."*

I

*Still fare the shadowy missioners across, by Dover-road
    and Calais Channel-track,*

II

*From Thames-side towers to Paris palace-gates ; from
    Paris leisurely to London back.*

I

*Till thus speaks France : " Much grief it gives us that,
    being pledged to treat, one Emperor with one King,*

II

*" You yet have struck a jarring counternote and tone that
    keys not with such promising.*

I

*" In these last words, then, of this pregnant parle ; I trust
    I may persuade your Excellency*

173

" That in no circumstance, on no pretence, a party to our pact can Russia be."

SPIRIT SINISTER

Fortunately for the manufacture of corpses by machinery Napoléon sticks to this veto, and so wards off the awkward catastrophe of a general peace descending upon Europe. Now England.

RUMOURS

(continuing)

I

Thereon speeds down through Kent and Picardy, evenly as some southing sky-bird's shade :

II

" We gather not from your Imperial lines a reason why our words should be reweighed.

I

" We hold to Russia not as our ally that is to be : she stands full-plighted so ;

II

" Thus trembles peace upon this balance-point : will you that Russia be let in or no ? "

I

Then France rolls out rough words across the strait :
" To treat with you confederate with the Tsar,

" *Presumes us sunk in sloughs of shamefulness from which*
     we yet stand gloriously afar !

" *The English army must be Flanders-flung, and entering*
     Picardy with pompous prance,

" *To warrant such !   Enough.   Our comfort is, the crime*
     of further strife lies not with France."

SPIRIT OF THE PITIES

Alas ! what prayer will save the struggling lands,
Whose lives are ninepins to these bowling hands ?

CHORUS OF RUMOURS

France secretly with — Russia plights her troth !
Britain, that lonely isle, is slurred by both.

SEA POWER

SEMICHORUS I OF IRONIC SPIRITS

(aerial music)

Deeming himself omnipotent
With the Kings of the Christian continent,
To warden the waves was his further bent.

SEMICHORUS II

But the weaving Will from eternity,
(Hemming them in by a circling sea)
Evolved the fleet of the Englishry.

SEMICHORUS I

The wane of his armaments ill-advised,
At Trafalgár, to a force despised,
Was a wound which never has cicatrized.

SEMICHORUS II

This, O this is the cramp that grips !
And freezes the Emperor's finger-tips
From signing a peace with the Land of Ships.

CHORUS

The Universal-empire plot
Demands the rule of that wave-walled spot ;
And peace with England cometh not !

AFTER JENA

CHORUS OF THE YEARS

(aerial music)

The prelude to this smooth scene — mark well ! — were
    the shocks whereof the times gave token
Vaguely to us ere last year's snows shut over Lithuanian
    pine and pool,
Which we told at the fall of the faded leaf, when the pride
    of Prussia was bruised and broken,
And the Man of Adventure sat in the seat of the Man of
    Method and rigid Rule.

SEMICHORUS I OF THE PITIES

Snows incarnadined were thine, O Eylau, field of the wide
    white spaces,
And frozen lakes, and frozen limbs, and blood iced hard
    as it left the veins :
Steel-cased squadrons swathed in cloud-drift, plunging to
    doom through pathless places,
And forty thousand dead and near dead, strewing the
    early-nighted plains.

SEMICHORUS II

Friedland to these adds its tale of victims, its midnight
    marches and hot collisions,
Its plunge, at his word, on the enemy hooped by the
    bended river and famed Mill stream,
As he shatters the moves of the loose-knit nations to curb
    his exploitful soul's ambitions,
And their great Confederacy dissolves like the diorama of
    a dream.

ALBUERA

SEMICHORUS I OF THE PITIES

(aerial music)

They come, beset by riddling hail ;
They sway like sedges in a gale ;
They fail, and win, and win, and fail.   *Albuera !*

SEMICHORUS II

They gain the ground there, yard by yard,
Their brows and hair and lashes charred,
Their blackened teeth set firm and hard.

SEMICHORUS I

Their mad assailants rave and reel,
And face, as men who scorn to feel,
The close-lined, three-edged prongs of steel.

SEMICHORUS II

Till faintness follows closing-in,
When, faltering headlong down, they spin
Like leaves.   But those pay well who win *Albuera.*

SEMICHORUS I

Out of six thousand souls that sware
To hold the mount, or pass elsewhere,
But eighteen hundred muster there.

SEMICHORUS II

Pale Colonels, Captains, ranksmen lie,
Facing the earth or facing sky ; —
They strove to live, they stretch to die.

SEMICHORUS I

Friends, foemen, mingle ; heap and heap. —
Hide their hacked bones, Earth ! — deep, deep, deep,
Where harmless worms caress and creep.

CHORUS

Hide their hacked bones, Earth ! — deep, deep, deep,
Where harmless worms caress and creep. —
What man can grieve ? what woman weep ?
Better than waking is to sleep !   Albuera !

EUROPE IN 1808

CHORUS OF THE YEARS

(aerial music)

Why watch we here ?   Look all around
Where Europe spreads her crinkled ground,
From Osmanlee to Hekla's mound,
                            Look all around !

Hark at the cloud-combed Ural pines ;
See how each, wailful-wise, inclines ;
Mark the mist's labyrinthine lines ;

Behold the tumbling Biscay Bay ;
The Midland main in silent sway ;
As urged to move them, so move they.

No less through regal puppet-shows
The rapt Determinator throes,
That neither good nor evil knows !

CHORUS OF THE PITIES

Yet It may wake and understand
Ere Earth unshape, know all things, and
With knowledge use a painless hand,
                            A painless hand !

RETREAT FROM MOSCOW

RECORDING ANGEL I

(in minor plain-song)

The host has turned from Moscow where it lay,
And Israel-like, moved by some master-sway,
Is made to wander on and waste away!

ANGEL II

By track of Tarutino first it flits;
Thence swerving, strikes at old Jaroslawitz;
The which, accurst by slaughtering swords, it quits.

ANGEL I

Harassed, it treads the trail by which it came,
To Borodino, field of bloodshot fame,
Whence stare unburied horrors beyond name!

ANGEL II

And so and thus it nears Smolensko's walls,
And, stayed its hunger, starts anew its crawls,
Till floats down one white morsel, which appals.

THE SERGEANT'S SONG

SONG: BUDMOUTH DEARS

I

When we lay where Budmouth Beach is,
O, the girls were fresh as peaches,
With their tall and tossing figures and their eyes of
blue and brown!
    And our hearts would ache with longing
    As we paced from our sing-songing,
With a smart *Clink! Clink!* up the Esplanade and
down.

II

    They distracted and delayed us
    By the pleasant pranks they played us,
And what marvel, then, if troopers, even of
regiments of renown,
    On whom flashed those eyes divine, O,
    Should forget the countersign, O,
As we tore *Clink! Clink!* back to camp above the
town.

III

    Do they miss us much, I wonder,
    Now that war has swept us sunder,
And we roam from where the faces smile to where
the faces frown?
    And no more behold the features
    Of the fair fantastic creatures,
And no more *Clink! Clink!* past the parlours of
the town?

IV

Shall we once again there meet them?
Falter fond attempts to greet them?
Will the gay sling-jacket [1] glow again beside the
       muslin gown? —
    Will they archly quiz and con us
    With a sideway glance upon us,
While our spurs *Clink! Clink!* up the Esplanade
       and down?

[1] Hussars, it may be remembered, used to wear a pelisse, dolman, or " sling-jacket " (as the men called it), which hung loosely over the shoulder. The writer is able to recall the picturesque effect of this uniform.

THE ALLIED SOVEREIGNS

SEMICHORUS I OF IRONIC SPIRITS

(aerial music)

We come ; and learn as Time's disordered deaf sands run
That Castlereagh's diplomacy has wiled, waxed, won.
The beacons flash the fevered news to eyes keen bent
That Austria's formal words of war are shaped, sealed,
  sent.

SEMICHORUS II

So ; Poland's three despoilers primed by Bull's gross pay
To stem Napoléon's might, he waits the weird dark day ;
His proffered peace declined with scorn, in fell force then
They front him, with yet ten-score thousand more massed
  men.

LEIPZIG I

SEMICHORUS I OF PITIES

Now, as in the dream of one sick to death,
  There comes a narrowing room
That pens him, body and limbs and breath,
  To wait a hideous doom,

SEMICHORUS II

So to Napoléon in the hush
  That holds the town and towers
Through this dire night, a creeping crush
  Seems inborne with the hours.

LEIPZIG II

SEMICHORUS I OF PITIES

(aerial music)

There leaps to the sky an earthen wave,
    And stones, and men, as though
Some rebel churchyard crew updrave
    Their sepulchres from below.

SEMICHORUS II

To Heaven is blown Bridge Lindenau ;
    Wrecked regiments reel therefrom ;
And rank and file in masses plough
    The sullen Elster-Strom.

SEMICHORUS I

A gulf is Lindenau ; and dead
    Are fifties, hundreds, tens ;
And every current ripples red
    With marshals' blood and men's.

SEMICHORUS II

The smart Macdonald swims therein,
    And barely wins the verge ;
Bold Poniatowski plunges in
    Never to re-emerge !

CHORUS OF IRONIC SPIRITS

The Battle of the Nations now is closing,
    And all is lost to One, to many gained ;
The old dynastic routine reimposing,
    The new dynastic structure unsustained.

Now every neighbouring realm is France's warder,
    And smirking satis₁action will be feigned :
The which is seemlier ? — so-called ancient order,
    Or that the hot-breath'd war-horse ramp unreined ?

ELBA

CHORUS OF RUMOURS
(aerial music)

Napoléon is going,
And nought will prevent him ;
He snatches the moment
Occasion has lent him !

And what is he going for,
Worn with war's labours ?
— To reconquer Europe
With seven hundred sabres.

Haste is salvation ;
And still he stays waiting :
The calm plays the tyrant,
His venture belating !

Should the corvette return
With the anxious Scotch colonel,
Escape would be frustrate,
Retention eternal.

The south wind, the south wind,
The south wind will save him,
Embaying the frigate
Whose speed would enslave him ;
Restoring the Empire
That fortune once gave him !

BEFORE WATERLOO

CHORUS OF THE YEARS

(aerial music)

The eyelids of eve fall together at last,
And the forms so foreign to field and tree
Lie down as though native, and slumber fast !

CHORUS OF THE PITIES

Sore are the thrills of misgiving we see
In the artless champaign at this harlequinade,
Distracting a vigil where calm should be !

The green seems opprest, and the Plain afraid
Of a Something to come, whereof these are the proofs,—
Neither earthquake, nor storm, nor eclipse's shade !

CHORUS OF THE YEARS

Yea, the coneys are scared by the thud of hoofs,
And their white scuts flash at their vanishing heels,
And swallows abandon the hamlet-roofs.

The mole's tunnelled chambers are crushed by wheels,
The lark's eggs scattered, their owners fled ;
And the hedgehog's household the sapper unseals.

The snail draws in at the terrible tread,
But in vain ; he is crushed by the felloe-rim ;
The worm asks what can be overhead,

And wriggles deep from a scene so grim,
And guesses him safe ; for he does not know
What a foul red flood will be soaking him !

Beaten about by the heel and toe
Are butterflies, sick of the day's long rheum,
To die of a worse than the weather-foe.

Trodden and bruised to a miry tomb
Are ears that have greened but will never be gold,
And flowers in the bud that will never bloom.

CHORUS OF THE PITIES

So the season's intent, ere its fruit unfold,
Is frustrate, and mangled, and made succumb,
Like a youth of promise struck stark and cold ! . .

And what of these who to-night have come ?

CHORUS OF THE YEARS

The young sleep sound ; but the weather awakes
In the veterans, pains from the past that numb ;

Old stabs of Ind, old Peninsular aches,
Old Friedland chills, haunt their moist mud bed,
Cramps from Austerlitz ; till their slumber breaks.

CHORUS OF SINISTER SPIRITS

And each soul sighs as he shifts his head
On the loam he's to lease with the other dead
From to-morrow's mist-fall till Time be sped !

AFTER WATERLOO

NAPOLÉON

(to himself, languidly)

Here should have been some troops of Gérard's
    corps,
Left to protect the passage of the convoys,
Yet they, too, fail. . . . I have nothing more to
    lose,
But life !

SPIRIT OF THE YEARS

" Sic diis immortalibus placet," —
" Thus is it pleasing to the immortal gods,"
As earthlings used to say. Thus, to this last,
The Will in thee has moved thee, Bonaparte,
As we say now.

NAPOLÉON

(starting)

        Whose frigid tones are those,
Breaking upon my lurid loneliness
So brusquely ? . . . Yet, 'tis true, I have ever
    known
That such a Will I passively obeyed !

SPIRIT IRONIC

Nothing care I for these high-doctrined dreams,
And shape the case in quite a common way,
So I would ask, Ajaccian Bonaparte,
Has all this been worth while ?

P

                              O hideous hour,
Why am I stung by spectral questionings?
Did not my clouded soul incline to match
Those of the corpses yonder, thou should'st rue
Thy saying, Fiend, whoever thou may'st be! . . .
    Why did the death-drops fail to bite me close
I took at Fontainebleau? Had I then ceased,
This deep had been unplumbed; had they but
        worked,
I had thrown threefold the glow of Hannibal
Down History's dusky lanes! — Is it too late? . . .
Yes. Self-sought death would smoke but damply
        here!
    If but a Kremlin cannon-shot had met me
My greatness would have stood: I should have
        scored
A vast repute, scarce paralleled in time.
As it did not, the fates had served me best
If in the thick and thunder of to-day,
Like Nelson, Harold, Hector, Cyrus, Saul,
I had been shifted from this jail of flesh,
To wander as a greatened ghost elsewhere.
— Yes, a good death, to have died on yonder field;
But never a ball came passing down my way!
    So, as it is, a miss-mark they will dub me;
And yet — I found the crown of France in the mire,
And with the point of my prevailing sword
I picked it up! But for all this and this
I shall be nothing. . . .
To shoulder Christ from out the topmost niche
In human fame, as once I fondly felt,

Was not for me. I came too late in time
To assume the prophet or the demi-god,
A part past playing now. My only course
To make good showance to posterity
Was to implant my line upon the throne.
And how shape that, if now extinction nears ?
Great men are meteors that consume themselves
To light the earth. This is my burnt-out hour.

SPIRIT OF THE YEARS

Thou sayest well. Thy full meridian shine
Was in the glory of the Dresden days,
When well-nigh every monarch throned in Europe
Bent at thy footstool.

NAPOLÉON

                    Saving always England's —
Rightly dost say " well-nigh." — Not England's, —
    she
Whose tough, enisled, self-centred, kindless craft
Has tracked me, springed me, thumbed me by the
    throat,
And made herself the means of mangling me !

SPIRIT IRONIC

Yea, the dull peoples and the Dynasts both,
Those counter-castes not oft adjustable,
Interests antagonistic, proud and poor,
Have for the nonce been bonded by a wish
To overthrow thee.

SPIRIT OF THE PITIES

> *Peace.   His loaded heart*
> *Bears weight enough for one bruised, blistered while !*

SPIRIT OF THE YEARS

Worthless these kneadings of thy narrow thought,
Napoléon ; gone thy opportunity !
Such men as thou, who wade across the world
To make an epoch, bless, confuse, appal,
Are in the elemental ages' chart
Like meanest insects on obscurest leaves
But incidents and grooves of Earth's unfolding ;
Or as the brazen rod that stirs the fire
Because it must.

THE END

SEMICHORUS I OF THE PITIES

(aerial music)

To Thee whose eye all Nature owns,
Who hurlest Dynasts from their thrones,[1]
And liftest those of low estate
We sing, with Her men consecrate !

SEMICHORUS II

Yea, Great and Good, Thee, Thee we hail,
Who shak'st the strong, Who shield'st the frail,
Who hadst not shaped such souls as we
If tendermercy lacked in Thee !

SEMICHORUS I

Though times be when the mortal moan
Seems unascending to Thy throne,
Though seers do not as yet explain
Why Suffering sobs to Thee in vain ;

SEMICHORUS II

We hold that Thy unscanted scope
Affords a food for final Hope,
That mild-eyed Prescience ponders nigh
Life's loom, to lull it by-and-by.

SEMICHORUS I

Therefore we quire to highest height
The Wellwiller, the kindly Might

[1] καθεῖλε ΔΥΝΑΣΤΑΣ ἀπὸ θρόνων.—Magnificat.

That balances the Vast for weal,
That purges as by wounds to heal.

SEMICHORUS II

The systemed suns the skies enscroll
Obey Thee in their rhythmic roll,
Ride radiantly at Thy command,
Are darkened by Thy Masterhand!

SEMICHORUS I

And these pale panting multitudes
Seen surging here, their moils, their moods,
All shall " fulfil their joy " in Thee,
In Thee abide eternally!

SEMICHORUS II

Exultant adoration give
The Alone, through Whom all living live,
The Alone, in Whom all dying die,
Whose means the End shall justify!   Amen.

SPIRIT OF THE PITIES

So did we evermore sublimely sing;
So would we now, despite thy forthshowing!

SPIRIT OF THE YEARS

Something of difference animates your quiring,
O half-convinced Compassionates and fond,
From chords consistent with our spectacle!

You almost charm my long philosophy
Out of my strong-built thought, and bear me back
To when I thanksgave thus. . . . Ay, start not, Shades;
In the Foregone I knew what dreaming was,
And could let raptures rule ! But not so now.
Yea, I psalmed thus and thus. . . . But not so now !

SEMICHORUS I OF THE YEARS

(aerial music)

O Immanence, That reasonest not
In putting forth all things begot,
Thou build'st Thy house in space — for what ?

SEMICHORUS II

O Loveless, Hateless ! — past the sense
Of kindly eyed benevolence,
To what tune danceth this Immense ?

SPIRIT IRONIC

For one I cannot answer. But I know
'Tis handsome of our Pities so to sing
The praises of the dreaming, dark, dumb Thing
That turns the handle of this idle Show !

As once a Greek asked [1] *I would fain ask too,*
Who knows if all the Spectacle be true,
Or an illusion of the gods (the Will,
To wit) some hocus-pocus to fulfil ?

---

[1] εἰ δ' ἐτήτυμος, τίς οἶδεν, ἤ τι θεῖόν ἐστι πη ψύθος; Aesch. *Agam.* 478.

SEMICHORUS I OF THE YEARS

(aerial music)

> *Last as first the question rings*
> *Of the Will's long travailings ;*
>> *Why the All-mover,*
>> *Why the All-prover*
> *Ever urges on and measures out the chordless chime of*
>> *Things.*[1]

SEMICHORUS II

> *Heaving dumbly*
> *As we deem,*
> *Moulding numbly*
> *As in dream,*
> *Apprehending not how fare the sentient subjects of Its*
>> *scheme.*

SEMICHORUS I OF THE PITIES

> *Nay ; — shall not Its blindness break ?*
> *Yea, must not Its heart awake,*
>> *Promptly tending*
>> *To Its mending*
> *In a genial germing purpose, and for loving-kindness' sake ?*

SEMICHORUS II

> *Should It never*
> *Curb or cure*
> *Aught whatever*
> *Those endure*
> *Whom It quickens, let them darkle to extinction swift and*
>> *sure.*

[1] Quid velit et possit rerum concordia discors ; Hor. *Epis.*
I. xii.

CHORUS

But — a stirring thrills the air
Like to sounds of joyance there
That the rages
Of the ages
Shall be cancelled, and deliverance offered from the darts
that were,
Consciousness the Will informing, till It fashion all
things fair !

INDEX TO FIRST LINES

THE END

PRINTED BY R. & R. CLARK, LTD., EDINBURGH